# WOODEN ACTION TOYS

# WOODEN ACTION TOYS

## BRYAN MAPSTONE

**DAVID & CHARLES**
Newton Abbot   London   North Pomfret (Vt)

This book is dedicated to Susan for her support and
acceptance of the countless lost hours while I was
writing it, and to Peter, Gemma and Rachel for letting
Daddy borrow back their toys

**British Library Cataloguing in Publication Data**
Mapstone, Bryan
 Wooden action toys.
 1. Wooden toy making
 I. Title
 745.592    TT174.5.W6

 ISBN 0–7153–9017–1

First published 1987
Second impression 1987

Phototypeset by ABM Typographics Limited, Hull
and printed in Great Britain
by Butler & Tanner Limited, Frome
for David & Charles Publishers plc
Brunel House   Newton Abbot   Devon

# CONTENTS

# ACKNOWLEDGEMENTS

I would like to acknowledge the help in getting *Wooden Action Toys* together from:
Maggs and Mac for the painting on the Play House; Mervyn of Data Powertools, Cardiff; Stanley Tools, Hand Tools Section; Record Marples Tools, Hand Tools Section; Britains Toys for the Farmyard and Dead Man's Gulch accessories; Black & Decker, Power Tools Section; Mattel Toys for Castle accessories; Matchbox Toys for Garage cars, etc; Hasbro Ltd; and finally Graham Sadd for his sympathetic ear.

# INTRODUCTION

Children's toys, as every parent knows, can be very expensive and they don't always last as long as you would like them to. So why not get back to some traditional standards and make your own toys? It is not as difficult as you might at first think. You will probably enjoy making them, and your children will definitely enjoy years of happy play with them. They may even become family heirlooms.

Homemade toys can cost next to nothing if they are made from bits and pieces that may be lying around in your garage, shed or workshop. In fact most of the toys featured in this book were made from scrap wood. The wheels for the pram were from an old pushchair that had seen better days.

Old furniture, cupboards, wardrobes, etc are a good source of reusable plywood, hardboard, wood, hinges, screws, etc.

All of the toys featured in this book have been made for my own children. They have been designed with strength and robustness in mind because children tend to use things in ways that they were never intended.

Some of the projects may seem a bit daunting to the beginner, but read through the instructions carefully, study the plans and everything will fall into place.

No complicated electrical power tools are needed to make these toys, but you will find an electrical jigsaw and drill very helpful items to have in your tool kit.

It may be said that beginners will have to kit themselves out with tools to make their first toy and therefore make the whole practice expensive. Initially this may be the case, but once you have a few tools at your disposal further projects can be made at no extra cost and it won't just stop at toys.

If a project does not turn out exactly as you had hoped, don't worry. Your child will not be looking for mistakes, only for a toy that has been made for them personally. I hope that you have as much enjoyment making the toys in this book as I have had and that your children get as much fun playing with them as my three children. Good Luck!

# UNDERSTANDING THE DRAWINGS

The first step to making any of the projects in this book is to understand the drawings. Each dimension contains two sets of figures eg 102(4). The number 102 represents millimetres (metric), the number in the brackets, (4), represents inches (imperial). Very often the metric number may not be an exact equivalent of the imperial number. Whichever system you choose to use, stick to it throughout. Using the metric system is not as difficult as might at first be thought; with practice you will probably find it easier to work with than all of those fractions of inches.

There are four different types of lines used on the drawings which may be confusing if you have never seen a mechanical drawing before:

1 *Continuous (thick)*
These denote the outline of a component that *can* be seen from the direction the drawing is viewed.
2 *Short dashes (thin)*
These denote the outline of an area that *can not* be seen from the direction the drawing is viewed. These lines then refer to hidden detail.
3 *Dashes broken by a dot*
These denote the centre line between two points or edges.
4 *Section lining (hatching)*
Thin parallel lines drawn at an angle of 45°. These denote the part of a component which remains after a portion is assumed to have been cut away and/or removed.

**Terms and abbreviations** used on drawings and cutting lists.

| | | |
|---|---|---|
| dia | – | Diameter |
| csk | – | Countersink |
| mm | – | Millimetres |
| in | – | Inches |
| rad | – | Radius |
| pitch | – | Fixing angle of a component |
| Ancillaries | – | Non-wooden components |

**Cutting lists**
The instructions for each toy include a cutting list for you to follow. It lists all the pieces required, with their exact dimensions. Not all the pieces have an accompanying drawing.

# METHODS AND MATERIALS

## Marking out

This is the first stage in any construction and it is where mistakes can easily happen. A sharp trimming or marking knife is ideal for marking out because they make a thin, easy-to-follow line. Use a pencil to shade areas that have to be removed when cutting out slots, tags and windows etc. Without this shading it is so easy to remove the wrong area. This is wasteful and time consuming.

## Materials

Nearly all of the projects in this book require plywood somewhere in their construction, and a better finish will be achieved if birch plywood is used. This is more expensive than ordinary plywood but it is of a higher quality and better suited to the rigours of child play. It is also a lot easier to paint because the grain is closer together.

Ordinary soft wood can be used for corner blocks and frame constructions etc. Hardwood should be used when making the cogs and latches for the castle or siege machines.

## Window and door openings

These are achieved by drilling two holes (which are large enough to accept your saw blade) in diagonal corners of the window, door etc to be removed. Insert a coping saw (jigsaw) blade into one of these holes, and cut to both of its adjoining corners. Remove the saw blade and insert it into the remaining hole; repeat the process. A file can then be used to smooth the edges of the opening.

## Sharpening chisels etc

Sharp tools are a must when working with wood and time spent sharpening them will be well rewarded. If you find it difficult to sharpen tools, there are honing guides available that will help you get a perfect edge. Always remember that blunt tools are dangerous.

## Countersinking

This is a method of getting a screw head below the level of the material it is screwed into. A drill bit the same diameter as the screw head can be used for this purpose, although an inexpensive countersink bit is preferable.

## Pilot holes

These are small holes which allow the insertion of a screw without splitting the surrounding material. A pilot hole should be smaller than the thread size of the screw used.

## Wheels

These can be made from hardwood using a hole cutter, or bought from commercial sources.

## Glue

Any glue which is specifically for wood should be used. Some glues are hard enough when dry to be sanded, and these will give you a second chance to remove unwanted glue. Contact adhesives should be avoided when bonding wood to wood.

## Cutting out

Whether you choose to use an electrical jigsaw or a hand saw to cut out your pieces, always secure your work firmly in a vice or to a bench or table with the appropriate cramps.

## Finishing off

Before any painting is attempted, use a fine grade abrasive paper to rub down your projects. Make sure that all edges are also smoothed off. This will reduce the risk of them splitting or tearing. Remove all dust from your project by using a cloth which has been damped with white spirit or turpentine substitute. After every coat of paint (except the final coat) lightly rub down your project with very fine abrasive paper. Only paints which are safe for children to handle should be used.

The drying time of paint is very dependent on temperature, and if you are painting your projects in a shed or garage during the winter months it is a good idea to bring them into the home overnight to allow them to dry properly.

A bad construction can be covered up with a good paint job, but a good construction can be ruined by a bad paint job. Don't be surprised if putting the finishing touches to your project takes longer than its construction. Any time spent on finishing is well worth any effort made.

Dry rub-on lettering can be used to improve a project, and use of an indelible marker pen will also add character and realism if lining is required as on the Castle and Alpha Space Fighter.

# HAND TOOLS: THEIR USES AND SAFETY

Although a lot of jobs these days are done with machines and computers, there is still a place for hand tools. They can be used anywhere and they are obviously not affected by electrical power cuts. Choosing hand tools must be given careful consideration, and buying a reputable brand of tool will pay dividends in the long run. A cheap tool may look identical to a more expensive one, but the difference will be in the quality of materials used and the method of manufacture, not just the brand name.

The following descriptions, uses and drawings of hand tools, were compiled with the help of Stanley Tools and Record Marples Tools. If you require any further information and help in choosing hand tools, Stanley Tools have prepared 36 fact sheets (to date) which are available free from some tool outlets. Or, consult a Record Marples Tools catalogue, which will also be free.

*Tenon or back saw*
Produces light accurate straight cuts either along or across a piece of wood, eg general bench work and cutting joints. The back keeps the blade rigid and may be made of brass or steel. Brass is generally found on top-quality saws.

*Hand saw*
Produces long straight cuts either along or across a piece of wood, eg cutting boards and sheet materials to size.

*Chisels (1)*
For general DIY use around the house you will need a minimum of three chisels: 6mm (¼in); 12mm (½in); 25mm (1in). Later, other sizes can be added. The firmer bevel edge chisel is the most versatile pattern. A chisel's main use is for removing waste wood. This can be to form a joint, or simply to shape the corner of a piece of wood.

*Spokeshave*
A spokeshave will enable you to shape curved surfaces both concave and convex as there are two types available; one for each type of curve.

*Bench plane (2)*
This is a tool which basically holds a 'chisel'-type blade firmly to make a controlled and accurate cut or shaving. This is achieved by allowing the blade to protrude very slightly through the sole of the plane, and the depth of cut adjustment and lateral adjusting lever control this.

There are many types and sizes of planes available, and some are for specialised tasks, eg cutting grooves, rebates or convex and concave curves.

In general, a smoothing plane with a sole length of 245mm (9¾in) and a cutter width of 50mm (2in) will be a good start to your tool kit.

*Honing guide*
An ideal accessory to help you sharpen chisels and plane blades to their correct angle.

*Marking gauge (3)*
Used for marking lines parallel to an edge with the grain.

*Mortise gauge*
Used for accurately marking out both mortise and tenons so that they are both the same.

*G cramp (4)*
These come in varying sizes and can be used for a variety of clamping jobs such as securing a piece of work to a bench or table, or securing two or more pieces of wood together while glue is allowed to harden.

*Sash cramps*
These are primarily designed for the cramping of large sections of work during joint glueing. With the addition of lengthening bars their capacity can be increased.

## Woodworker's bench vice
Available in varying sizes and costs, they are as invaluable to the amateur as they are to the professional. Some vices are fitted with a very useful quick release mechanism.

## Joiner's mallet (5)
Should be used for chiselling and assembly operations in preference to a steel hammer so that damage does not occur to your chisel or work piece.

## Bradawl (6)
For starting screw holes to prevent splitting the wood.

## Hand drill (7)
Used for accurate drilling of small diameter holes.

## Countersink bit (8)
To enable a screw head to sit flush with the surface of the wood, screw holes must be countersunk using this special bit.

## Flat bit (9)
Designed specifically for use with an electric drill it bores holes quickly, cleanly and safely in all types of wood and many other materials. A minimum drill speed of 1,000 rpm is recommended by Marples Ridgway Tools Ltd and all size flat bits work efficiently at 2,500 rpm.

## Combination square (10)
An all-purpose square it will mark out both 90° and 45° angles. The sliding head can be locked in any position to check surfaces and angles. It can also be used as a rule.

## Sliding bevel
This is a try-square which can be adjusted and locked to any angle for marking angles or checking angular surfaces.

## Mitre block or box (11)
Both of these are used as a saw guide for cutting angles of 45°.

## Bench hook
For helping to secure wood when sawing with a tenon or back saw.

## Claw hammer (12)
Ideal for heavy nailing jobs and the removal of old nails.

## Warrington hammer (13)
Suitable for light joinery work, ie picture framing, fixing wallboards to battens, securing hardboard/plywood etc.

## Stanley knife
There are many different types of this knife available, and which to choose is a matter of personal preference, but the retractable blade knife should be considered for safety reasons. Uses of these knives are too numerous and varied to list, but they are very useful when marking cross grain lines because they cut the wood's fibres cleanly and finely. If fitted with a wood cutting blade, the knife will double up as a keyhole saw.

## Flexible steel tape measure
These are available in different lengths and will measure both metric and imperial. Most blades are replaceable to increase the life of the rule. Do not use these rules for marking straight lines.

## Hand tools safety check list
It is not only power tools that are a potential danger to their users. Hand tools if not used correctly can also be dangerous. Always ask advice from your tool supplier if you are not sure of something, or visit your local library for a book dealing specifically with the use of tools. Below is a short list of safety hints which you may find helpful.

*Never*

1 Never use a tool for any purpose other than that for which it is designed.
2 Never use the side of a hammer to strike metal objects.
3 Never use a hammer which has a dirty face as it will tend to slip.
4 Never use tools that are broken or damaged. Repair properly or replace.
5 Never push metal objects in the mouth of a plane to release jammed shavings.
6 Never use a flexible steel tape measure as a guide when marking with a sharp knife.
7 Never stand a plane upright as damage

to the blade may occur.

8 Never test the sharpness of any blade, chisel etc by applying direct pressure to the edge with fingers or thumb.

*Always*

1 Always use sharp chisels, planes etc. Blunt tools require more effort for them to cut, and are therefore less controllable.

2 Always, when using any type of saw, start your cut slowly using your thumb nail as a guide. When the saw cut has started, move your steadying hand well clear of the blade in case it jumps out.

3 Always use a solid steel straight-edge when marking with a Stanley knife.

4 Always secure your piece of work firmly to a bench, table or vice before carrying out any work on it.

5 Always keep tools out of reach of children.

6 Always ensure that your work area is clean and tidy.

# POWER TOOLS: THEIR USES AND SAFETY

Power tools are a great aid to have in a home workshop. Experience in their use has to be learnt as with hand tools, but when this experience has been gained, power tools will help you to carry out many jobs in and around your home more quickly and easily.

Choosing a power tool to suit a particular need can be difficult for both the beginner and experienced craftsman alike. Your local dealer should be able to help you make the choice that is right for you.

There are two main categories of power tools available, DIY and professional. DIY tools have been developed for the occasional home user and are more than adequate for this purpose. Professional tools are designed for continuous and more rigorous uses in various professions.

Linking these two main categories however, is the Black & Decker Power Plus range. This range of tools combines qualities that are found in both DIY and professional tools.

When you have decided how much work you are going to have for a particular tool, this will then dictate the class of tool to be bought, ie DIY, Power Plus or professional.

The following drawings, descriptions and uses of power tools have been compiled with the help of Black & Decker Power Tools Ltd and are only intended to be a brief guide. If any further information is required, this should be available from a power tool stockist.

*Electric drill (1)*
This is probably the most widely used of all power tools. Electronic speed control which is available on some models will enable you to drill holes in most materials and start drilling holes at slower speeds for greater accuracy.

*Vertical drill stand*
Where accuracy is essential in drilling holes at exactly 90° to the horizontal, a

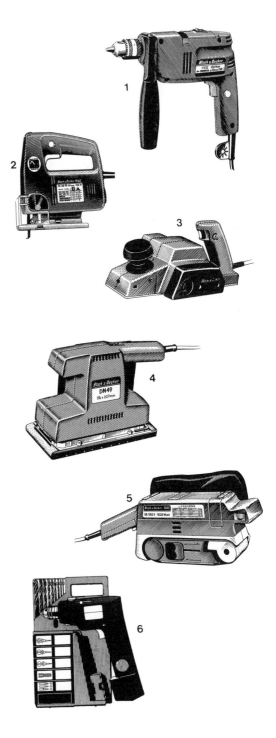

vertical drill stand is indispensable. When using the depth gauge on the drill stand, fine adjustment can be achieved for exact drilling depth. A machine vice can also be fitted which will help when drilling small or round objects.

### Jigsaw (2)

By changing the blade and speed of a jigsaw to suit the material to be cut, it can be a very useful and versatile power tool. The 'sole' of a jigsaw can be adjusted so that it will cut angles of between 45° and 90°. An electronic pendulum orbital jigsaw which has a dust-blower and plunger safety guard, is ideally suited to most work you will have to do.

### Planing machine (3)

A planing machine will enable you to turn a rough piece of waste wood into a smooth re-usable work piece with the minimum fuss. Used inverted with a bench support and blade guard, the planing machine can be operated for stationary work and small work pieces. Cutting rebates can also be done by using a parallel guide and setting the depth gauge. Very useful when making the wallboard surrounds (see page 30).

### Orbital sander (4)

Generally used for finishing work. By adjusting the speed of an electronic orbital sander and using different grade abrasive papers, it is possible to use it for sanding materials like heat sensitive plastics, and for removing old paint.

### Belt sander (5)

Generally used for heavy duty sanding. If inverted and bench mounted, a belt sander can be used very successfully in the workshop for sharpening tools and more importantly to sand and shape work pieces.

### Cordless drill/screwdriver (6)

Cordless power gives you the chance to do DIY tasks in places you could never reach with conventional power drills. There are no restricting power cables to snag or trip over so it makes life a little bit easier when working in confined spaces such as a shed

or small workroom. Because of their slow speed they are excellent for screw-driving. The recharge time of cordless drills/screwdrivers can vary, but an average time is approximately 1 hour.

### Power tools safety check list

Most accidents with power tools that happen to people occur in and around the home, so care must be taken when using them to minimise any potential danger. If you have any worries about using power tools, most tool dealers will provide helpful assistance and possibly provide a demonstration.

*Never*

1 Never carry a power tool around if it is switched on and running.
2 Never wear loose clothing or ties while operating power tools.
3 Never make adjustments to power tools while they are plugged in.
4 Never leave a power tool plugged in and unattended.
5 Never use accessories which are not designed for your power tool.
6 Never use a power tool for any purpose other than that for which it is designed.

*Always*

1 Always read the manufacturer's literature before operating an unfamiliar power tool.
2 Always ensure that the floor area you are working in is clean and tidy.
3 Always wear sound footwear.
4 If your machine has a lock ON switch, always make sure it is in the OFF position before plugging it in.
5 If you have long hair, always tie it up out of the way.
6 Always keep power cables free from obstructions and saw blades etc. If a power tool is continually used for bench work, chaffing can occur on the power cable so check regularly for wear.
7 When using accessories, always ensure they are right for your machine and that they are adjusted correctly.
8 Always wear protective clothing etc where appropriate; eg safety goggles and dust masks.

# FARMYARD

*(shown in colour on page 52)*

This farmyard is an excellent toy with which to start a young child's imagination working. There are so many possibilities of play themes that can be different every day and give a child many hours of enjoyment.

The solid construction of the buildings will give many years of faithful service, and they have already been 'tested' by my own children.

1 Construction can begin anywhere, but you will find it easier if you follow the cutting list.
2 The walls on the baseboard (Figs 1 and 2) are interlocked with each other, and are glued and pinned to the base. I chose to paint the walls, but dolls' house brick paper can be used.
3 When making the pig sty (Fig 3), glue the inside wall in position before pinning and glueing the roof.
4 It is important to glue and pin 9×9mm (³⁄₈×³⁄₈in) battens of varying lengths to the base and inside corners of the farmhouse (Fig 5) to give strength to the walls.
5 Before fixing the roof to the house, cut to length some more 9×9mm (³⁄₈×³⁄₈in) battens and glue them to the top inside edges.
6 When painting the finished farmyard only use paints that are lead-free.

## Cutting list

| | | | |
|---|---|---|---|
| Baseboard (Fig 1) | 1 off | 490×490×3mm (19¹⁄₄×19¹⁄₄×¹⁄₈in) | Hardboard |
| Walls (Fig 2) | 2 off | 490×18×12mm (19¹⁄₄×³⁄₄×¹⁄₂in) | Plywood |
| | 4 off | 177×18×12mm (7×³⁄₄×¹⁄₂in) | Plywood |

*Pig sty* (Fig 3)

| | | | |
|---|---|---|---|
| Base | 1 off | 118×152×3mm (4⁵⁄₈×6×¹⁄₈in) | Plywood |
| Side walls | 2 off | 50×152×9mm (2×6×³⁄₈in | Plywood |
| Front wall | 1 off | 18×118×9mm (³⁄₄×4⁵⁄₈×³⁄₈in) | Plywood |
| Back wall | 1 off | 50×118×9mm (2×4⁵⁄₈×³⁄₈in | Plywood |
| Inside wall | 1 off | 50×38×3mm (2×1¹⁄₂×¹⁄₈in) | Plywood |
| Roof | 1 off | 70×118×3mm (2³⁄₄×4⁵⁄₈×¹⁄₈in) | Hardboard |

*Cow shed* (Fig 4)

| | | | |
|---|---|---|---|
| Base | 1 off | 102×162×3mm (4×6³⁄₈×¹⁄₈in) | Plywood |
| Side walls | 2 off | 102×102×9mm (4×4×³⁄₈in) | Plywood |
| Back wall | 1 off | 79×162×9mm (3¹⁄₈×6³⁄₈×³⁄₈in) | Plywood |
| Stalls | 2 off | 25×92×9mm (1×3⁵⁄₈×³⁄₈in) | Plywood |
| Roof | 1 off | 172×112×4mm (6³⁄₄×4³⁄₈×³⁄₁₆in) | Hardboard |

*Farmhouse* (Fig 5)

| | | | |
|---|---|---|---|
| Base | 1 off | 102×162×4mm (4×6³⁄₈×³⁄₁₆in) | Plywood |
| Front/rear walls | 2 off | 102×162×4mm (4×6³⁄₈×³⁄₁₆in) | Plywood |
| End walls | 2 off | 152×102×4mm (6×4×³⁄₁₆in) | Plywood |
| Base board battens | 2 off | 154×9×9mm (6×³⁄₈×³⁄₈in) | Wood |
| | 2 off | 94×9×9mm (3⁵⁄₈×³⁄₈×³⁄₈in) | Wood |
| Roof | 1 off | 172×75×4mm (6³⁄₄×2¹⁵⁄₁₆×³⁄₁₆in) | Plywood |
| | 1 off | 172×79×4mm (6³⁄₄×3¹⁄₈×³⁄₁₆in) | Plywood |

Various sized 9×9mm (³⁄₈×³⁄₈in) blocks glued to inside of walls and roof for added strength

## Fig 1 Baseboard

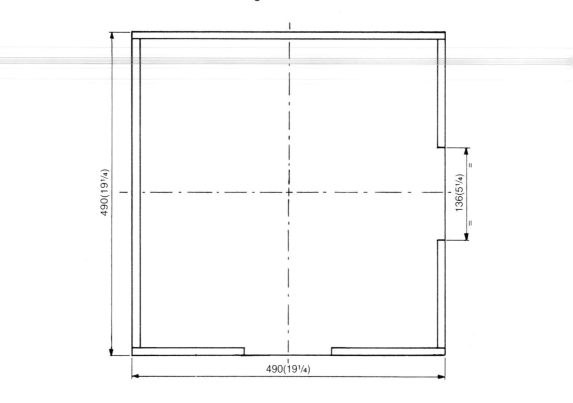

490(19¼)

490(19¼)

136(5¼)

## Fig 2 Walls
### make two, 12(½) thick

466(18¼)

9(³/₈)

18(³/₄)

490(19¼)

### make four, 12(½) thick

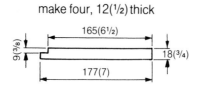

165(6½)

9(³/₈)

18(³/₄)

177(7)

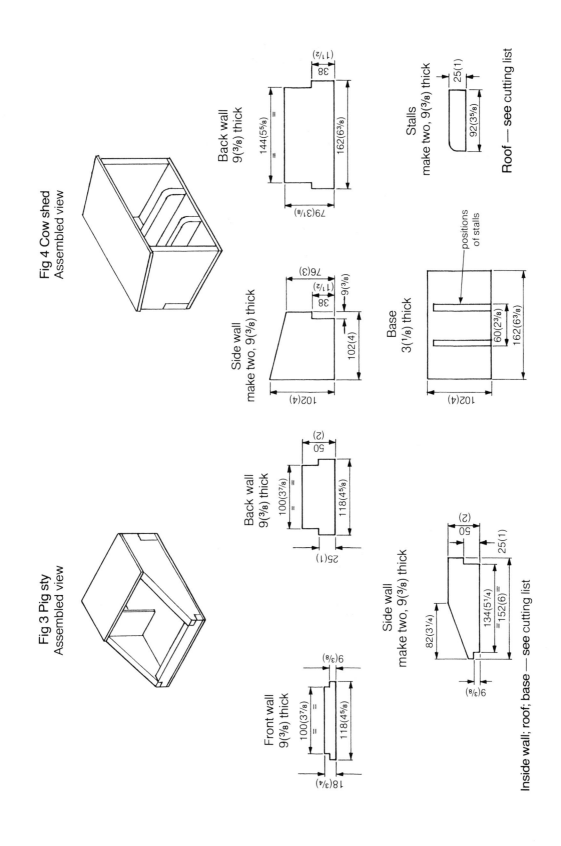

Fig 4 Cow shed
Assembled view

Back wall
9(³/₈) thick

144(5⁵/₈)
162(6³/₈)
38
(1¹/₂)
79(3¹/₈)

Stalls
make two, 9(³/₈) thick

25(1)
92(3⁵/₈)

Roof — see cutting list

Side wall
make two, 9(³/₈) thick

76(3)
38
(1¹/₂)
9(³/₈)
102(4)
102(4)

Base
3(¹/₈) thick

positions of stalls

60(2³/₈)
162(6³/₈)
102(4)

Fig 3 Pig sty
Assembled view

Back wall
9(³/₈) thick

50
(2)
100(3⁷/₈)
118(4⁵/₈)
25(1)

Side wall
make two, 9(³/₈) thick

50
(2)
25(1)
82(3¹/₄)
134(5¹/₄)
= 152(6) =
9(³/₈)

Front wall
9(³/₈) thick

9(³/₈)
100(3⁷/₈)
118(4⁵/₈)
18(³/₄)

Inside wall; roof; base — see cutting list

# Fig 5 Farmhouse
## Assembled view

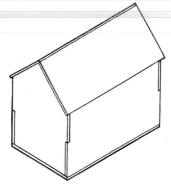

### End walls
### make two, 4(³/₁₆) thick

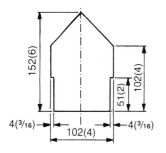

152(6)  51(2)  102(4)  4(³/₁₆)  102(4)  4(³/₁₆)

### Front / rear walls
### make one of each 4(³/₁₆) thick

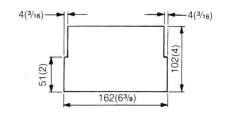

4(³/₁₆)  4(³/₁₆)  51(2)  102(4)  162(6³/₈)

### Base
### 4(³/₁₆) thick

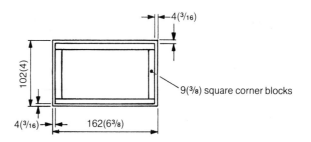

4(³/₁₆)  102(4)  9(³/₈) square corner blocks  4(³/₁₆)  162(6³/₈)

# STICK PUPPET

*(shown in colour on page 34)*

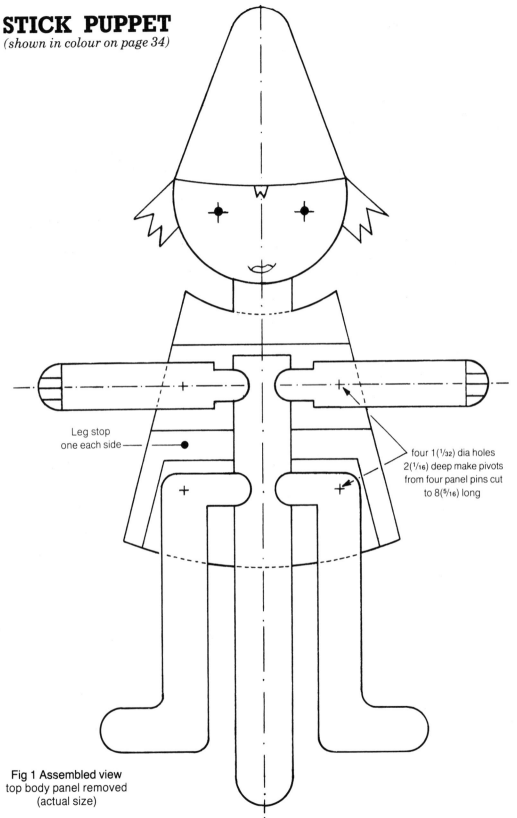

Leg stop
one each side

four 1(¹⁄₃₂) dia holes
2(¹⁄₁₆) deep make pivots
from four panel pins cut
to 8(⁵⁄₁₆) long

Fig 1 Assembled view
top body panel removed
(actual size)

## Fig 2 Head
### 4(³/₁₆) thick

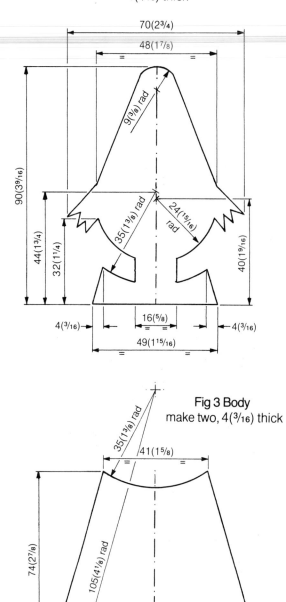

70(2³/₄)
48(1⁷/₈)
9(³/₈) rad
90(3⁹/₁₆)
44(1³/₄)
32(1¹/₄)
35(1³/₈) rad
24(¹⁵/₁₆) rad
40(1⁹/₁₆)
4(³/₁₆)
16(⁵/₈)
4(³/₁₆)
49(1¹⁵/₁₆)

## Fig 4 Arm
### make two, 4(³/₁₆) thick

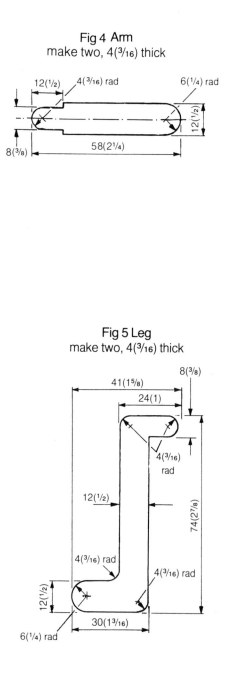

12(¹/₂)
4(³/₁₆) rad
6(¹/₄) rad
12(¹/₂)
8(³/₈)
58(2¹/₄)

## Fig 3 Body
### make two, 4(³/₁₆) thick

35(1³/₈) rad
41(1⁵/₈)
74(2⁷/₈)
105(4¹/₈) rad
79(3¹/₈)

## Fig 5 Leg
### make two, 4(³/₁₆) thick

41(1⁵/₈)
24(1)
8(³/₈)
4(³/₁₆) rad
12(¹/₂)
4(³/₁₆) rad
74(2⁷/₈)
4(³/₁₆) rad
12(¹/₂)
30(1³/₁₆)
6(¹/₄) rad

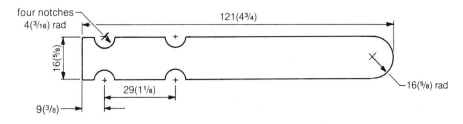

Fig 6 Operating stick
4(³/₁₆) thick

four notches
4(³/₁₆) rad

121(4³/₄)

16(⁵/₈)

29(1¹/₈)

9(³/₈)

16(⁵/₈) rad

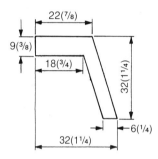

Fig 7 Leg stop
make two, 4(³/₁₆) thick

22(⁷/₈)

9(³/₈)

18(³/₄)

32(1¹/₄)

6(¹/₄)

32(1¹/₄)

1 Mark and cut out two body sections (Fig 3). As will be seen in Fig 1, each body section has to have four 1mm (¹/₃₂in) dia holes 2mm (¹/₁₆in) deep drilled into it. This can easily be done using tracing paper to transfer their positions to the body sections.

2 Mark and cut out the head (Fig 2) and two leg stops (Fig 7). Glue them in position on one body section as shown (Fig 1).

3 Mark and cut out two arms (Fig 4), two legs (Fig 5) and the operating stick (Fig 6). The notches on the operating stick can be made using a round file.

4 Place the arms, legs and operating stick in position on the body section which has the head and leg stops already glued to it. Using the tracing paper that has the pivot hole positions marked on it, transfer these positions to the legs and arms and drill the four 1mm (¹/₃₂in) dia holes.

5 Make the pivots by cutting four panel pins each to a length of 8mm (⁵/₁₆in). Place the pivots through the arm, leg and body pivot holes. Place the remaining body section onto the assembled body section and test the operation of the puppet.

6 When satisfied with the operation of the puppet, carefully glue the body sections together, making sure that all moving parts remain free of glue. If there is any stiffness with the operating stick etc, use candle wax to ease it.

7 To make the puppet move, push the operating stick up and down.

### Cutting list

| | | | |
|---|---|---|---|
| Head (Fig 2) | 1 off | 90×70×4mm (3⁹/₁₆×2³/₄×³/₁₆in) | Plywood |
| Body (Fig 3) | 2 off | 79×74×4mm (3¹/₈×2⁷/₈×³/₁₆in) | Plywood |
| Arms (Fig 4) | 2 off | 58×12×4mm (2¹/₄×¹/₂×³/₁₆in) | Plywood |
| Legs (Fig 5) | 2 off | 74×41×4mm (2⁷/₈×1⁵/₈×³/₁₆in) | Plywood |
| Operating stick (Fig 6) | 1 off | 121×16×4mm (4³/₄×⁵/₈×³/₁₆in) | Plywood |
| Leg stop (Fig 7) | 2 off | 32×32×4mm (1¹/₄×1¹/₄×³/₁₆in) | Plywood |

# SUPERSONIC AIRLINER

*(shown in colour on page 87)*

With this project children can fly their own supersonic airliner. Admittedly champagne and caviar will not be on the menu, but this project does have the advantage of being able to be made from scrap bits and pieces that may be lying around your garage or workshop.

When it is finished, you can take your pick of colour schemes from a whole world of airlines, many of them very colourful.

1 Start by shaping the fuselage (Fig 1) and drilling the 9mm (3/8in) diameter holes for the windows using a flat bit (*see* page 13).

Drill the holes partly through from one side first, only marking the underside with the drill point. When all holes have been partly drilled, turn the fuselage over and complete the drilling.

2 Cut out tail and wing sections (Figs 2 and 3).

3 Mark the position of the tail section on the fuselage, and using a 6mm (1/4in) dia drill bit, make a slot 12mm (1/2in) deep. Remove waste wood with a small chisel and test fit tail section.

4 Mark the position of the wing section on the underside of the fuselage and remove waste wood using a coping saw. Test fit wing section, cleaning recess if required.

5 Glue tail section in position, then glue and pin wing section in position, making sure that the pins will not protrude through the window openings.

6 Cut out and glue engines (Fig 4) in position.

7 When all glue has hardened, round off all edges and paint.

## Cutting list

| | | | |
|---|---|---|---|
| Fuselage (Fig 1) | 1 off | 365×35×18mm (14 3/8 × 1 3/8 × 3/4in) | Wood |
| Tail section (Fig 2) | 1 off | 63×63×6mm (2 1/2 × 2 1/2 × 1/4in) | Plywood |
| Wing section (Fig 3) | 1 off | 184×171×6mm (7 1/4 × 6 3/4 × 1/4in) | Plywood |
| Engines (Fig 4) | 2 off | 53×32×12mm (2 1/8 × 1 1/4 × 1/2in) | Wood |

## Fig 1 Fuselage
### Side view

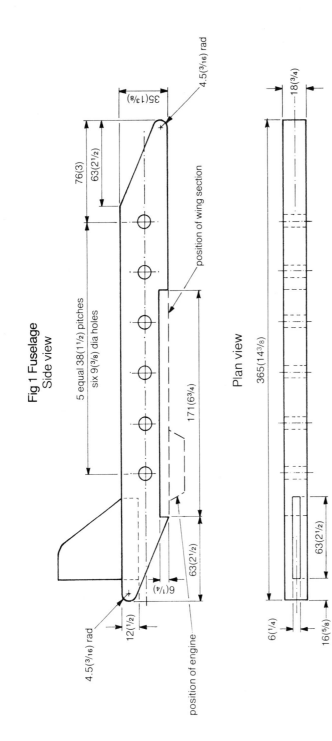

5 equal 38(1½) pitches
six 9(³⁄₈) dia holes

35(1³⁄₈)

76(3)

63(2½)

4·5(³⁄₁₆) rad

position of wing section

171(6³⁄₄)

63(2½)

6(¼)

4·5(³⁄₁₆) rad

12(½)

position of engine

## Plan view

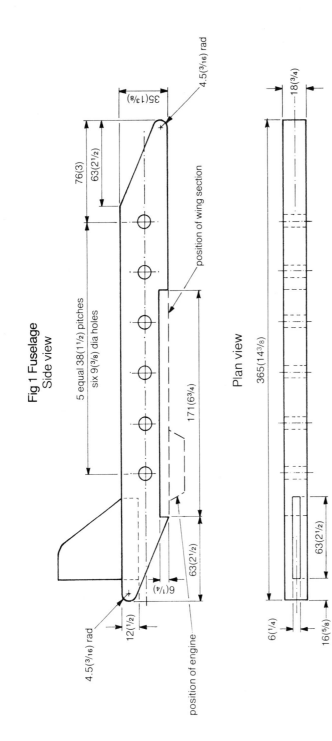

18(³⁄₄)

365(14³⁄₈)

63(2½)

6(¼)

16(⁵⁄₈)

## Fig 2 Tail section
6(¼) thick

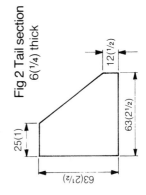

12(½)

25(1)

63(2½)

63(2½)

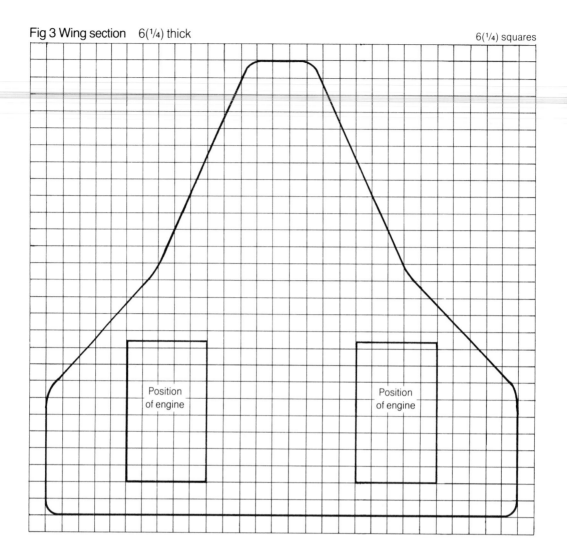

**Fig 3 Wing section**  6(¼) thick

6(¼) squares

Position of engine

Position of engine

**Fig 4 Engines**
make two, 12(½) thick

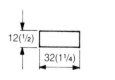

12(½)

32(1¼)

53(2⅛)

41(1⅝)

# ALPHA SPACE FIGHTER

*(shown in colour on page 87)*

As with the Supersonic Airliner (page 24) the Alpha Space Fighter is yet another project that can turn small offcuts of wood into a very presentable model.

Why not make two or three Alpha Space Fighters? Paint them different colours and imaginary dog fights fought many galaxies away will become reality here on earth.

1 Mark and cut out the wing section (Fig 4). Drill three 9mm (³⁄₈in) dia holes as shown.

2 Cut to length the two fuselages (Fig 5). Before any shaping is done, drill three 9mm (³⁄₈in) dia holes in each fuselage as shown.

3 The tail sections (Fig 6) on each fuselage are slotted in at an angle. To achieve this a small jig has to be made (as shown in Fig 7) so that both fuselages can be drilled at the same angle.

Mark the position of the tail sections on each fuselage, clamp each fuselage in turn to the jig, and with your drill in a vertical position drill a series of 6mm (¹⁄₄in) dia holes, 6mm (¹⁄₄in) deep to form each slot.

Finish shaping both fuselages and glue the dowels and tail sections in position.

4 Cut out and shape the two main body sections (Figs 8 and 9).

Drill an 18mm (³⁄₄in) dia hole, 6mm (¹⁄₄in) deep in the upper section. Then pin and glue the two sections together.

5 The 'droid' (*see* Fig 1) which is glued into the upper body section is made from 18mm (³⁄₄in) dia dowel, 16mm (⁵⁄₈in) long.

It is easier to shape this part before cutting it to length.

6 Test assemble, then pin and glue the fuselages and main body sections to the wings.

7 Cut three 12mm (¹⁄₂in) long, 9mm (³⁄₈in) dia dowels and glue them in position on the underside of the wing section to form the landing gear (*see* Fig 2).

8 To improve the finished appearance of the Alpha Space Fighter, water slide decals from plastic aeroplane kits can be used.

Use a clear varnish to paint over any decals used. This will help to protect them from lazer cannon fire etc.

**Cutting list**

| | | | |
|---|---|---|---|
| Wing section (Fig 4) | 1 off | 178×102×6mm (7×4×¹⁄₄in) | Plywood |
| Fuselages (Fig 5) | 2 off | 158×32×16mm (6¹⁄₄×1¹⁄₄×⁵⁄₈in) | Wood |
| Tail sections (Fig 6) | 2 off | 38×28×6mm (1¹⁄₂×1¹⁄₈×¹⁄₄in) | Plywood |
| Rear dowels (top) | 2 off | 30mm(1³⁄₁₆in)long×9mm(³⁄₈in)dia dowel | |
| (bottom) | 2 off | 35mm(1³⁄₈in)long×9mm(³⁄₈in)dia dowel | |
| Front dowels (Fig 3) | 2 off | 57mm(2¹⁄₄in)long×9mm(³⁄₈in)dia dowel | |
| Main body | | | |
| (lower section) (Fig 8) | 1 off | 50×102×12mm (2×4×¹⁄₂in) | Wood |
| (upper section) (Fig 9) | 1 off | 28×96×12mm (1¹⁄₈×3³⁄₄×¹⁄₂in) | Wood |
| Droid (Fig 1) | 1 off | 18mm(³⁄₄in)long×18mm(³⁄₄in)dia dowel | |
| Landing gear (Fig 2) | 3 off | 12mm(¹⁄₂in)long×9mm(³⁄₈in)dia dowel | |
| Fuselage drilling jig | | | |
| (Fig 7) | 2 off | 102×35×18mm (4×1³⁄₈×³⁄₄in) | Wood |
| | 1 off | 102×108×6mm (4×4¹⁄₄×¹⁄₄in) | Plywood |

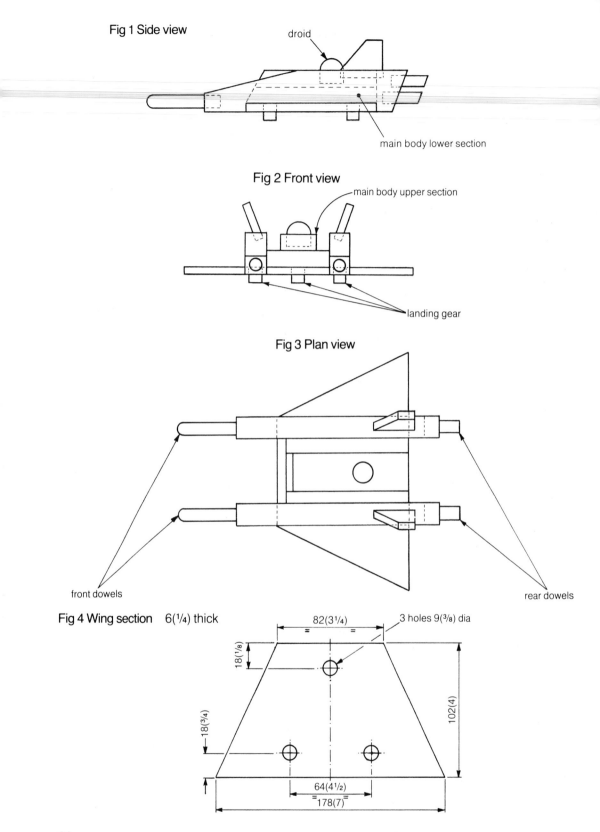

Fig 1 Side view

droid

main body lower section

Fig 2 Front view

main body upper section

landing gear

Fig 3 Plan view

front dowels

rear dowels

**Fig 4 Wing section**   6(¹/₄) thick

82(3¹/₄)

3 holes 9(³/₈) dia

18(¹/₈)

18(³/₄)

102(4)

64(4¹/₂)

178(7)

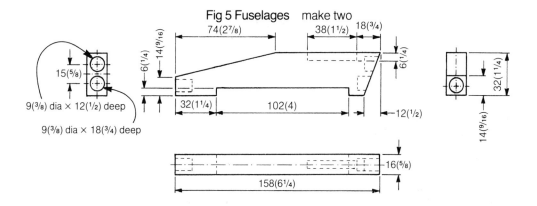

Fig 5 Fuselages   make two

74(2⁷⁄₈)   38(1¹⁄₂)   18(³⁄₄)

14(⁹⁄₁₆)

6(¹⁄₄)

6(¹⁄₄)

32(1¹⁄₄)

15(⁵⁄₈)

9(³⁄₈) dia × 12(¹⁄₂) deep

9(³⁄₈) dia × 18(³⁄₄) deep

32(1¹⁄₄)   102(4)   12(¹⁄₂)

14(⁹⁄₁₆)

16(⁵⁄₈)

158(6¹⁄₄)

Fig 6 Tail section   make two, 6(¹⁄₄) thick

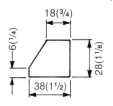

18(³⁄₄)

6(¹⁄₄)

28(1¹⁄₈)

38(1¹⁄₂)

Fig 7 Fuselage drill jig
assembled side view

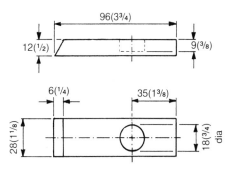

102 × 108 × 6
(4 × 4¹⁄₄ × ¹⁄₄)
plywood

two blocks
102 × 35 × 18(4 × 1³⁄₈ × ³⁄₄)

Fig 8 Main body — lower section

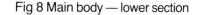

102(4)

12(¹⁄₂)

6(¹⁄₄)

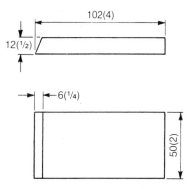

50(2)

Fig 9 Main body — upper section

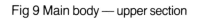

96(3³⁄₄)

12(¹⁄₂)

9(³⁄₈)

6(¹⁄₄)   35(1³⁄₈)

28(1¹⁄₈)

18(³⁄₄)
dia

# PINBOARDS

*(shown in colour on page 34)*

Children of all ages like to 'decorate' their own bedrooms with photographs and magazine cuttings of their favourite sport and pop personalities, etc. This can be a bit of a headache for the decorator of the household as it doesn't do the wallpaper a lot of good when posters are changing position all the time.

Here is a simple solution to torn wallpaper which enables the individual to alter his/her board as often as they wish. If there is more than one child in the family, it is a good idea to paint the surrounding rails in different colours and use matching drawing pins for the photographs, etc.

1 Cut each side rail to length with a 45° mitre at each end facing the centre (Figs 1 and 2).
2 Drill the appropriate number of 5mm (3/16in) holes in each rail (Fig 1).
3 Using a marking gauge, mark the position of the 12mm(½in)wide×9mm(3/8in) deep rebate (Fig 3) on each rail and remove. This rebate can be cut out in a

number of ways:
*a* using a hand rebate planer
*b* an electric power planer
*c* a router
*d* circular saw

When using any of these methods it is important to adjust the tool used correctly. A piece of scrap wood should be used as a test piece.
4 Radius the top corners of each rail and smooth off.
5 Cut the pinboard to size and smooth off any rough edges.
6 You will find it easier and cleaner to paint the rails and pinboard before fixing it to the wall.
7 To fit the board to the wall, first screw the bottom rail (with the aid of a spirit level) in the required position, using bright zinc screws and cup washers. Now screw into position one of the two vertical rails. Do not tighten any fixing screws at this point. Slide the pinboard into position and tighten the rail fixing screws. Now screw the remaining two rails in position.

**Cutting list**

| Side rails (Fig 1) | 2 off | 1651×38×18mm (65×1½×¾in) | Wood |
|---|---|---|---|
| (Fig 2) | 2 off | 660×38×18mm (26×1½×¾in) | Wood |
| | 1 off | 1625×635×9mm (64×25×3/8in) | Pinboard |

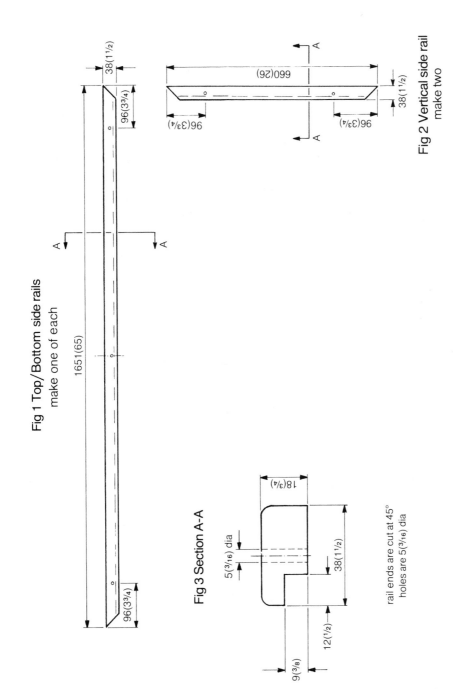

Fig 1 Top/Bottom side rails
make one of each

38(1½)

96(3¾)

1651(65)

96(3¾)

A

A

Fig 2 Vertical side rail
make two

660(26)

38(1½)

96(3¾)

96(3¾)

A

A

Fig 3 Section A-A

18(¾)

5(³⁄₁₆) dia

38(1½)

12(½)

9(⅜)

rail ends are cut at 45°
holes are 5(³⁄₁₆) dia

# DEAD MAN'S GULCH

*(shown in colour opposite)*

Who said 'cowboys are dead' and 'everyone's gone to the moon'? Nonsense! They are all alive and well living in Dead Man's Gulch, complete with a jail, general store, full hotel and empty bank.

All of the buildings in Dead Man's Gulch have been designed to the same scale as the plastic cowboys and indians that are found in most children's toy-boxes with nowhere of their own to live.

Why not try your children with a new angle to cowboys and indians? Let them imagine that Dead Man's Gulch is a film set and that they are directing a brand new block buster film, all about the legendary Billy the Kid.

Getting back to reality for a moment we first have to build our town.

1 Cut to size all the 6mm (¼in) thick plywood panels which will make up each building. Most of the panels have slots and/or tags on them. These tags ensure that when the buildings are finally assembled they slot together like a 3-dimensional jigsaw.

2 When cutting out the windows refer to the introductory section at the front of the book (see page 9).

3 When you have cut out enough panels for the buildings you are making, test assemble and then glue and cramp them in position.

4 *Sheriff's office/Bank* The side windows are only cut out on the bank model and the beds (Fig 21) are only fitted into the sheriff's office. The horse rail (Fig 20) can be fitted on opposite sides of the bases with these two models to add variety.

5 *Livery stable* The side roofs (*see* cutting list) have to have their edges shaped to fit in with the side walls and the top flat roof. This is done after the top flat roof has been glued in position. If desired 9mm (³⁄₈in) square blocks can be glued to inside corners for added strength.

6 *Hotel* This is cut out and assembled in the same way as the other buildings. When drilling the holes for the pillars, place the balcony over the base (flat together) and drill through both parts as one. Beds can also be fitted inside this model as in the Sheriff's Office, if desired.

## Cutting list

*Sheriff's office/Bank*

| | | | |
|---|---|---|---|
| Base (Fig 1) | 1 off | 203×152×6mm (8×6×¼in) | Plywood |
| Front wall (Fig 2) | 1 off | 152×108×6mm (6×4¼×¼in) | Plywood |
| Side walls (Fig 3) | 2 off | 114×102×6mm (4½×4×¼in) | Plywood |
| Roof | 1 off | 140×108×6mm (5½×4¼×¼in) | Plywood |
| Roof supports/ corner blocks | 4 off | 76×9×9mm (3×³⁄₈×³⁄₈in) | Wood |
| Beds (Fig 21) | 2 off | 57×25×18mm (2¼×1×¾in) | Wood |
| Pillows | 2 off | 18×9×3mm (¾×⅞×⅛in) | Plywood |
| Horse rail (Fig 20) | 2 off | 45×12×6mm (1¾×½×¼in) | Plywood |
| | 1 off | 45mm(1¾in)long×4mm(³⁄₁₆in)dia dowel | |

*Livery stable*

| | | | |
|---|---|---|---|
| Base (Fig 4) | 1 off | 213×140×6mm (8³⁄₈×5½×¼in) | Plywood |
| Front wall (Fig 5) | 1 off | 213×184×6mm (8³⁄₈×7¼×¼in) | Plywood |

*Railway (see page 118) and Dead Man's Gulch (above)*

mummy

| | | | |
|---|---|---|---|
| Back wall (Fig 6) | 1 off | 213×166×6mm (8³⁄₈×6¹⁄₂×¹⁄₄in) | Plywood |
| Side walls (Fig 7) | 2 off | 140×124×6mm (5¹⁄₂×4⁷⁄₈×¹⁄₄in) | Plywood |
| Top flat roof (Fig 8) | 1 off | 140×92×6mm (5¹⁄₂×3⁵⁄₈×¹⁄₄in) | Plywood |
| Side roof | 2 off | 134×76×6mm (5¹⁄₄×3×¹⁄₄in) | Plywood |
| Hoist beam | 1 off | 45×9×9mm (1³⁄₄×³⁄₈×³⁄₈in) | Wood |

*Hotel*

| | | | |
|---|---|---|---|
| Base (Fig 9) | 1 off | 277×178×6mm (10⁷⁄₈×7×¹⁄₄in) | Plywood |
| Front wall (Fig 10) | 1 off | 213×184×6mm (8³⁄₈×7¹⁄₄×¹⁄₄in | Plywood |
| Side walls (Fig 11) | 2 off | 140×184×6mm (5¹⁄₂×7¹⁄₄×¹⁄₄in) | Plywood |
| First floor (Fig 12) | 1 off | 237×152×6mm (9³⁄₈×6×¹⁄₄in) | Plywood |
| Balcony (Fig 13) | 1 off | 277×178×6mm (10⁷⁄₈×7×¹⁄₄in) | Plywood |
|     Front rail (Fig 14) | 1 off | 277×32×6mm (10⁷⁄₈×1¹⁄₄×¹⁄₄in) | Plywood |
|     Side rails (Fig 15) | 2 off | 178×32×6mm (7×1¹⁄₄×¹⁄₄in) | Plywood |
|     End panels | 2 off | 26×26×6mm (1×1×¹⁄₄in) | Plywood |
| Pillars | 4 off | 95mm(3³⁄₄in)long×9mm(³⁄₈in)dia dowel | |
| Roof | 1 off | 210×134×6mm (7⁷⁄₈×5¹⁄₄×¹⁄₄in) | Plywood |
| Roof support/ corner blocks | 4 off | 76×9×9mm (3×³⁄₈×³⁄₈in) | Wood |
| Horse rail (Fig 20) | 2 off | As Sheriff's office/Bank | |
| Beds (Fig 21) | | As Sheriff's office/Bank (if required) | |

*General store/barber's*

| | | | |
|---|---|---|---|
| Base (Fig 16) | 1 off | 383×178×6mm (15¹⁄₈×7×¹⁄₄in) | Plywood |
| Front wall (Fig 17) | 1 off | 333×102×6mm (13¹⁄₈×4×¹⁄₄in) | Plywood |
| Side walls (Fig 18) | 2 off | 146×102×6mm (5¹⁄₄×4×¹⁄₄in) | Plywood |
| Inside wall (Fig 19) | 1 off | 146×84×6mm (5³⁄₄×3¹⁄₄×¹⁄₄in) | Plywood |
| Roof | 1 off | 321×140×6mm (12⁵⁄₈×5¹⁄₂×¹⁄₄in) | Plywood |
| Roof supports/ corner blocks | 4 off | 76×9×9mm (3×³⁄₈×³⁄₈in) | Wood |
| Horse rails (Fig 20) | 1 or 2 | As Sheriff's office/Bank (if required) | |

*Water trough* (Fig 22)

| | | | |
|---|---|---|---|
| Base | 1 off | 18×50×6mm (³⁄₄×2×¹⁄₄in) | Plywood |
| Sides | 2 off | 18×18×6mm (³⁄₄×³⁄₄×¹⁄₄in) | Plywood |
| | 2 off | 18×62×6mm (³⁄₄×2¹⁄₂×¹⁄₄in) | Plywood |
| Stand pipe | 1 off | 38×12×6mm (1¹⁄₂×¹⁄₂×¹⁄₄in) | Plywood |
| | | 18mm(³⁄₄in)long×4mm(³⁄₁₆in)dia dowel | |

*Pinboard (see page 30) and Stick Puppet (see page 21)*

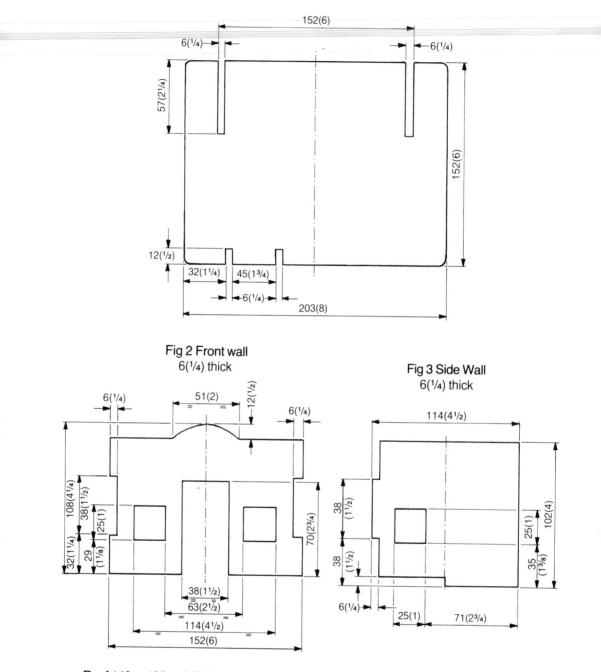

**Fig 1 Base**
6($\frac{1}{4}$) thick

152(6)

6($\frac{1}{4}$)　　　　　6($\frac{1}{4}$)

57(2$\frac{1}{4}$)

152(6)

12($\frac{1}{2}$)

32(1$\frac{1}{4}$)　45(1$\frac{3}{4}$)

6($\frac{1}{4}$)

203(8)

**Fig 2 Front wall**
6($\frac{1}{4}$) thick

**Fig 3 Side Wall**
6($\frac{1}{4}$) thick

6($\frac{1}{4}$)　　51(2)　　12($\frac{1}{2}$)

6($\frac{1}{4}$)

114(4$\frac{1}{2}$)

108(4$\frac{1}{4}$)　38(1$\frac{1}{2}$)　25(1)

32(1$\frac{1}{4}$)　29(1$\frac{1}{8}$)

70(2$\frac{3}{4}$)

38(1$\frac{1}{2}$)

38(1$\frac{1}{2}$)

25(1)

102(4)

35(1$\frac{3}{8}$)

38(1$\frac{1}{2}$)
63(2$\frac{1}{2}$)
114(4$\frac{1}{2}$)
152(6)

6($\frac{1}{4}$)　25(1)　71(2$\frac{3}{4}$)

Roof 140 × 108 × 6(5$\frac{1}{2}$ × 4$\frac{1}{4}$ × $\frac{1}{4}$)
Roof support/corner blocks　make four, 76 × 9 × 9 (3 × $\frac{3}{8}$ × $\frac{3}{8}$)

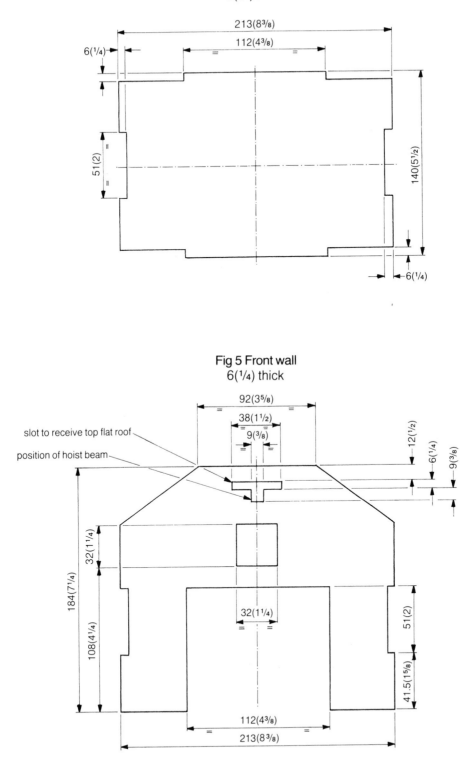

**Fig 4 Base**
6(¼) thick

213(8³⁄₈)

112(4³⁄₈)

6(¼)

=                                =

51(2)

=

140(5½)

6(¼)

**Fig 5 Front wall**
6(¼) thick

92(3⁵⁄₈)

=                                =

38(1½)

=                    =

9(³⁄₈)

=          =

slot to receive top flat roof

position of hoist beam

12(½)

6(¼)

9(³⁄₈)

184(7¼)

32(1¼)

108(4¼)

32(1¼)

=          =

51(2)

41.5(1⁵⁄₈)

112(4³⁄₈)

=                    =

213(8³⁄₈)

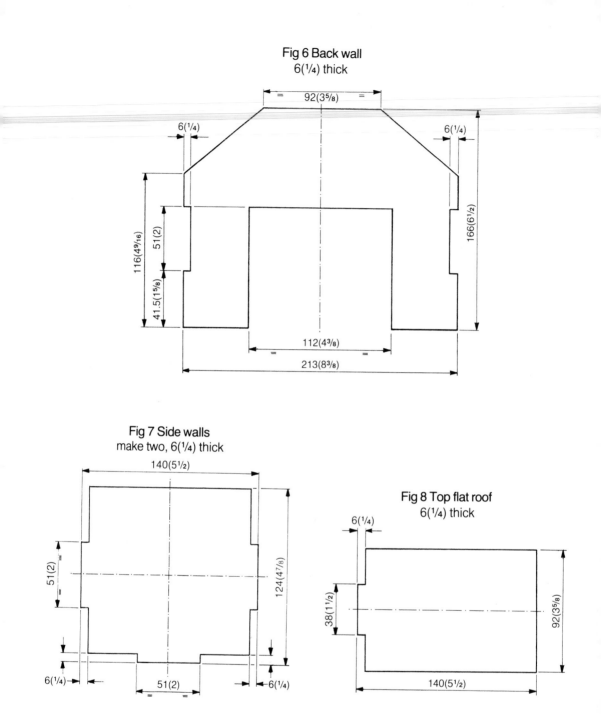

Fig 6 Back wall
6(¼) thick

Fig 7 Side walls
make two, 6(¼) thick

Fig 8 Top flat roof
6(¼) thick

Hoist beam 45 × 9 × 9(1¾ × ⅜ × ⅜)
Side roofs  make two 134 × 76 × 6(5¼ × 3 × ¼)  angle edges to fit

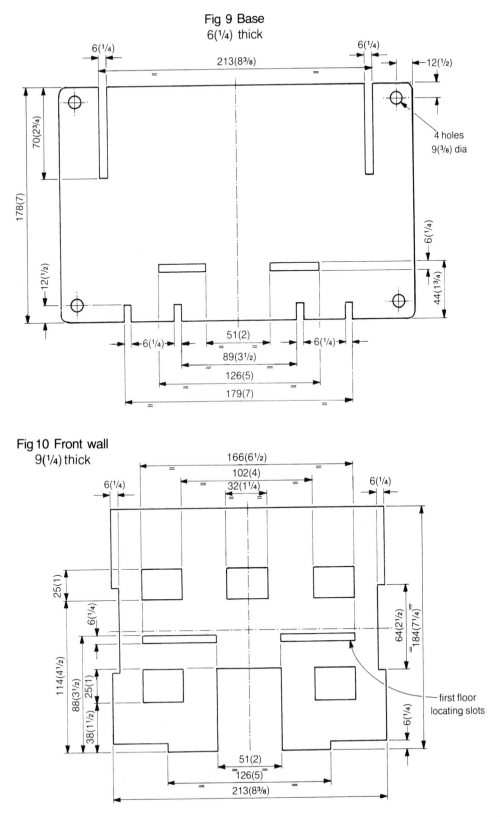

**Fig 9 Base**
6(¼) thick

6(¼)
6(¼)
213(8³/₈)
12(½)
70(2³/₄)
178(7)
12(½)
4 holes
9(³/₈) dia
6(¼)
44(1³/₄)
6(¼)
51(2)
6(¼)
89(3½)
126(5)
179(7)

**Fig 10 Front wall**
9(¼) thick

166(6½)
102(4)
32(1¼)
6(¼)
6(¼)
25(1)
6(¼)
64(2½)
184(7¼)
114(4½)
88(3½)
25(1)
38(1½)
first floor
locating slots
6(¼)
51(2)
126(5)
213(8³/₈)

## Fig 11 Side wall
make two, 6(¼) thick

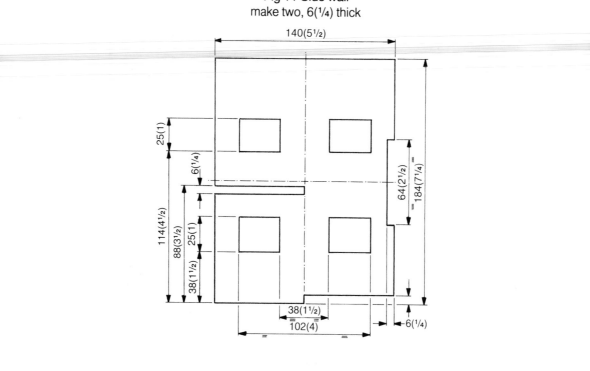

## Fig 12 First floor
6(¼) thick

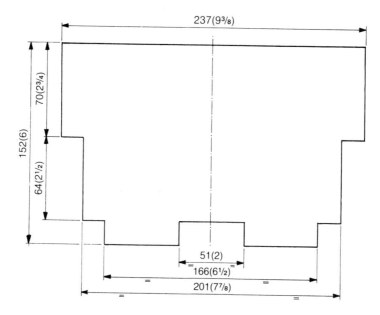

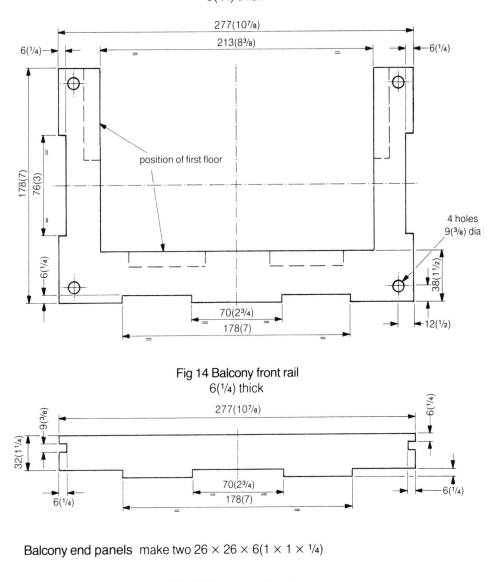

## Fig 13 Balcony
### 6(¼) thick

277(10⁷/₈)

213(8³/₈)

6(¼)

6(¼)

178(7)

76(3)

6(¼)

position of first floor

4 holes
9(³/₈) dia

38(1¹/₂)

70(2³/₄)

178(7)

12(¹/₂)

## Fig 14 Balcony front rail
### 6(¼) thick

277(10⁷/₈)

9(³/₈)

32(1¹/₄)

6(¼)

6(¼)

70(2³/₄)

178(7)

6(¼)

6(¼)

**Balcony end panels** make two 26 × 26 × 6(1 × 1 × ¼)

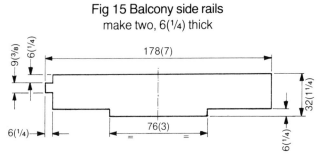

## Fig 15 Balcony side rails
### make two, 6(¼) thick

178(7)

9(³/₈)

6(¼)

32(1¹/₄)

6(¼)

76(3)

6(¼)

**Roof** 201 × 134 × 6(7⁷/₈ × 5¹/₄ × ¼)
**Roof support/corner blocks** make four 76 × 9 × 9(3 × ³/₈ × ³/₈)

# Fig 16 Base
### 6(¼) thick

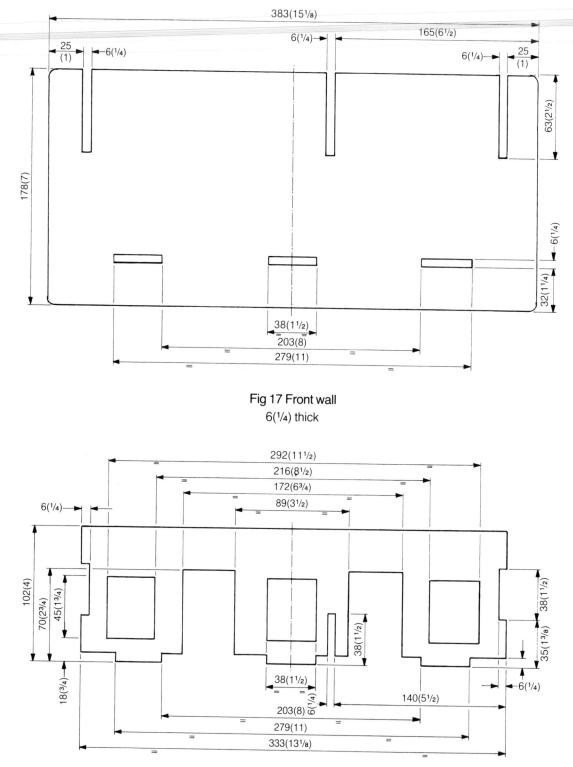

# Fig 17 Front wall
### 6(¼) thick

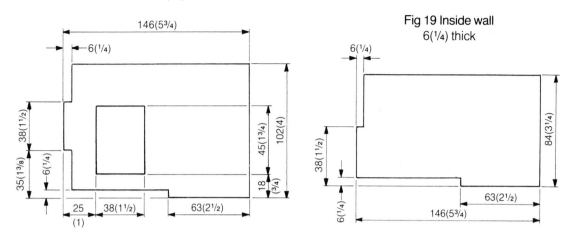

Fig 18 Side walls
make two, 6(¼) thick

146(5¾)
6(¼)
38(1½)
35(1⅜)
6(¼)
45(1¾)
102(4)
18 (¾)
25 (1)
38(1½)
63(2½)

Fig 19 Inside wall
6(¼) thick

6(¼)
38(1½)
6(¼)
84(3¼)
63(2½)
146(5¾)

Roof supports/corner blocks  make four 76× 9 × 9(3 × ⅜ × ⅜)
Roof  321 × 140 × 6(12⅝ × 5½ × ¼)

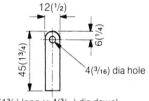

Fig 20 Horse rail
make two, 6(¼) thick

12(½)
45(1¾)
6(¼)
4(³⁄₁₆) dia hole
45(1¾) long × 4(³⁄₁₆) dia dowel
joins the two uprights

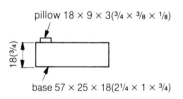

Fig 21 Beds
make two

pillow 18 × 9 × 3(¾ × ⅜ × ⅛)
18(¾)
base 57 × 25 × 18(2¼ × 1 × ¾)

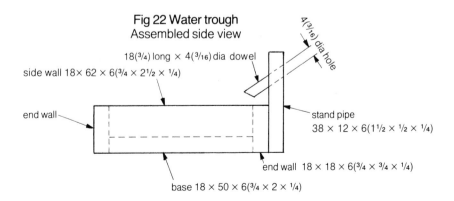

Fig 22 Water trough
Assembled side view

4(³⁄₁₆) dia hole
18(¾) long × 4(³⁄₁₆) dia dowel
side wall 18× 62 × 6(¾ × 2½ × ¼)
end wall
stand pipe
38 × 12 × 6(1½ × ½ × ¼)
end wall  18 × 18 × 6(¾ × ¾ × ¼)
base 18 × 50 × 6(¾ × 2 × ¼)

# DOLL'S PRAM
*(shown in colour on page 51)*

Playing with dolls in various situations is all part of growing up for young girls. They change them, feed them, bath them and put them to bed etc, just as their parents do with them.

They associate their play very strongly with the real world and no child's formative years would be complete without a pram that they could be taken for walks in on a sunny day.

Likewise, every 'young mother' would like her own pram to take her 'baby' for walks.

Any 'young mother' will be proud to take her 'baby' for a walk in this pram. With its built-in shopping tray she can even pick up a few groceries while she is out.

To enhance the appearance of this pram, the talents of somebody who is good at sewing should be enlisted so that matching pillows and covers can be made.

1 Before any construction can commence a compass has to be made that will draw a radius of 200mm (7⅞in). This is a very simple task and it can be made from any

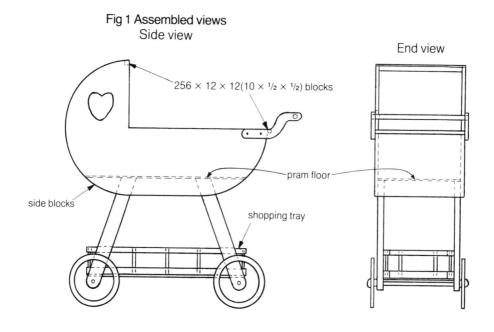

Fig 1 Assembled views
Side view

256 × 12 × 12(10 × ½ × ½) blocks

side blocks

pram floor

shopping tray

End view

Plan view
shopping tray not shown

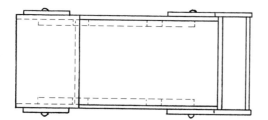

## Fig 2 Sides
make two, 12(½) thick

635(25)

400(15¾)

200(7⅞) rad

200(7⅞) rad

92 (3⅝)

256(10¹/₁₆)

368(14½)

six 3(⅛) dia leg and side block fixing holes countersunk

## Fig 4 Side blocks
make two sets 18(¾) thick

276(10⅞)

184(7¹/₁₆)

51(2)

218(8⁹/₁₆)

310(12³/₁₆)

500(19¹¹/₁₆)

## Fig 3 Heart
6(¼) squares

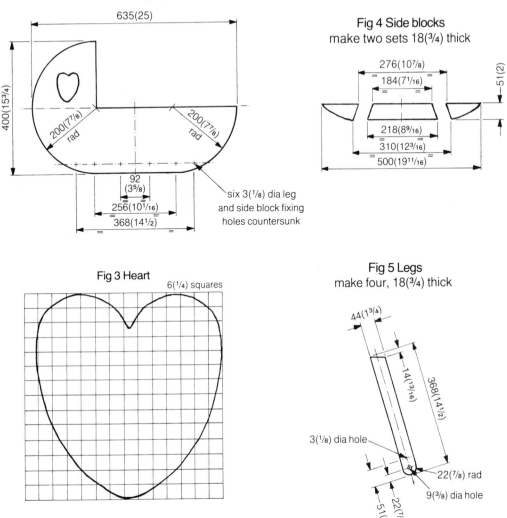

## Fig 5 Legs
make four, 18(¾) thick

44(1¾)

14(¹³/₁₆)

368(14½)

3(⅛) dia hole

22(⅞) rad

9(⅜) dia hole

51(2)

22(⅞)

piece of scrap wood which is longer than 200mm (7⅞in). Drive a nail through one end of the wood which will act as the point of our compass.

Drill a 6mm (¼in) hole, 200mm (7⅞in) distance from the nail point. This hole is for the pencil to be used and it must be a tight fit.

2 Now that the compass has been made the two pram sides (Fig 2) can be marked and cut.

The heart shape (Fig 3) should be en-larged by drawing a grid of 6mm (¼in) squares, and transferring the parts of the design contained in each of the squares in Fig 3 to the enlarged grid.

3 Clamp the finished sides together and sand the edges until both are the same. Drill and countersink the leg and side block fixing holes at this stage.

4 The side blocks (Fig 4) that are fitted to the inside of each pram side are now cut to length. *Do not* cut them into three parts at this stage. Place each of them in position

45

on the sides, mark where they overlap the curve and remove the waste wood using a coping saw.

When this has been done, they can be marked where they are to be cut into three. Now screw the un-cut side blocks in position on the pram sides and transfer the markings from the side blocks to the pram sides.

After marking, remove the side blocks and cut each into three parts. The cut side blocks should now be screwed and glued into position.

5 Make the four legs (Fig 5) and test assemble them into the slots between the side blocks.

Again we need to mark through the pram sides into each leg so that when they are eventually screwed and glued in position the task will be easier. Remove all legs after test assembly.

6 Cut out the hardboard floor (*see* Fig 1) and pin and glue it in position on top of the side blocks.

7 The next stage is to cut out and fit the 1.5mm ($^1/16$in) thick plywood (Figs 6 and 7) which will wrap around the edges of the pram sides.

When marking out, the grain *must* run across the width of the pram, otherwise it will not bend to the required shape.

Cutting is easiest if done with a sharp trimming knife.

Because one sheet of 1.5mm ($^1/16$in) thick plywood is not strong enough on its own, two sheets slightly different in length have to be sandwiched together.

When glueing the first piece in position (the shortest), use panel pins to hold it in place but *do not* drive them all the way in as they have to be removed before the second piece can be glued on top of the first.

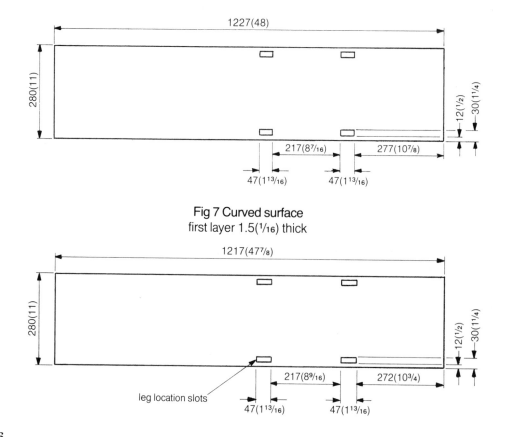

Fig 6 Curved surface
second layer 1.5($^1/16$) thick

Fig 7 Curved surface
first layer 1.5($^1/16$) thick

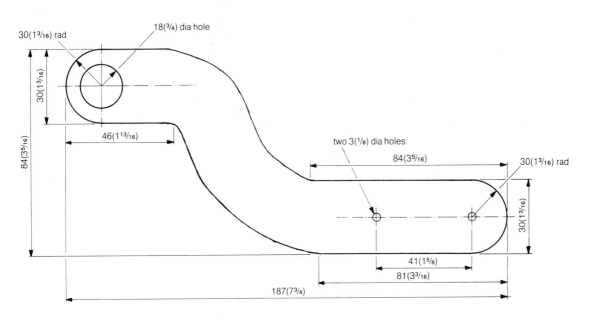

**Fig 8 Handles**
make two, 12(½) thick

30(1³/₁₆) rad

18(¾) dia hole

30(1³/₁₆)

84(3⁵/₁₆)

46(1¹³/₁₆)

two 3(⅛) dia holes

84(3⁵/₁₆)

30(1³/₁₆) rad

30(1³/₁₆)

41(1⅝)

81(3³/₁₆)

187(7¾)

## Fig 9 Shopping tray

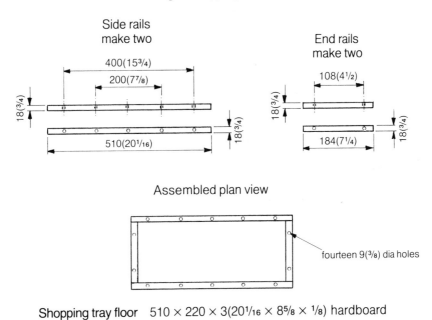

Side rails
make two

400(15¾)

200(7⅞)

18(¾)

18(¾)

510(20¹/₁₆)

End rails
make two

108(4½)

18(¾)

18(¾)

184(7¼)

Assembled plan view

fourteen 9(⅜) dia holes

Shopping tray floor   510 × 220 × 3(20¹/₁₆ × 8⅝ × ⅛) hardboard

Ensure there is an even covering of adhesive on the first panel before attempting to put the second panel in place.

8 Glue and pin the two 12×12mm (½×½in) blocks in position. These will give protection to the thin plywood edges.

9 Screw and glue legs in position.

10 Mark and cut out the handles (Fig 8), using the methods described in section 2 above for the heart shape.

Screw and glue them in position, and glue and pin the handle-bar in position for added strength. Make sure the pins are given an extra tap with a nail punch so they will not catch little fingers.

11 Make up the shopping tray (Fig 9) using a flat bit to drill the holes. Drill half way through each batten from one side first, then drill the rest of the hole from the other side where the centre has been marked by the drill bit. This will stop the wood from tearing around the hole.

When completed screw the tray to the legs. It will be necessary to remove the tray for painting.

12 Using glass paper smooth off all edges. It is advisable to paint the pram before fitting the axles and wheels.

13 Cut the axles to length and fit them in place. A flat washer with an internal dia of 9mm (⅜in) should be fitted behind each wheel against its respective leg.

## Cutting list

| | | | |
|---|---|---|---|
| Sides (Fig 2) | 2 off | 635×400×12mm (25×15¾×½in) | Plywood |
| Side blocks (Fig 4) | 2 sets made from | 1000×51×18mm (39⅜×2×¾in) | Wood |
| Legs (Fig 5) | 4 off | 368×44×18mm (14½×1¾×¾in) | Wood |
| Pram floor | 1 off | 502×256×3mm (19¾×10¹/₁₆in×⅛in) | Hardboard |
| Curved surface (Fig 7) | 1 off | 1217×280×1.5mm (47⅞×11×¹/₁₆in) | Birch plywood |
| (Fig 6) | 1 off | 1227×280×1.5mm (48⁵/₁₆×11×¹/₁₆in) | Birch plywood |
| Wood blocks | 1 off | 256×12×12mm (10¹/₁₆×½×½in) | Wood |
| | 1 off | 280×12×12mm (11×½×½in) | Wood |
| Handles (Fig 8) | 2 off | 187×84×12mm (7⅜×3⁵/₁₆×½in) | Plywood |
| Handle bar | 1 off | 304mm(12in)long×18mm(¾in)dia dowel | |
| Shopping tray side rails (Fig 9) | 4 off | 510×18×18mm (20¹/₁₆×¾×¾in) | Wood |
| | 4 off | 184×18×18mm (7¼×¾×¾in) | Wood |
| | 14 off | 86mm(3⅜in)long×9mm(¾in)dia dowel | |
| Shopping tray floor | 1 off | 510×220×3mm (20¹/₁₆×8⅝×⅛in) | Hardboard |

*Ancillaries*

| | | | |
|---|---|---|---|
| Axles | 2 off | 340(13⅜in)long×9mm(⅜in)dia steel rod | |
| Spring dome caps | 4 off | To fit 9mm(⅜in)dia steel rod | |
| Wheels | 4 off | 152mm(6in)dia, axle size 9mm(⅜in) | |
| Brass washers | 4 off | Internal dia of 9mm(⅜in) 12mm(½in)long, 17 gauge panel pins | |

# SHOP/PUPPET THEATRE

*(shown in colour on page 51)*

Here is an excellent place for children to learn about the real world of buying, selling and getting used to handling money.

Empty food boxes and containers can be used to add realism, but don't use glass jars or bottles. If you have a friendly local shop keeper, he may let you have some paper bags.

While watching my children, they seem to enjoy putting things in and taking things out of paper bags, and selling me my shopping. I would recommend their prices to anyone, they must be the cheapest around.

With the addition of three short lengths of plastic curtain track screwed to the top batten of each arch wall, and some small curtains, the shop now becomes a puppet theatre.

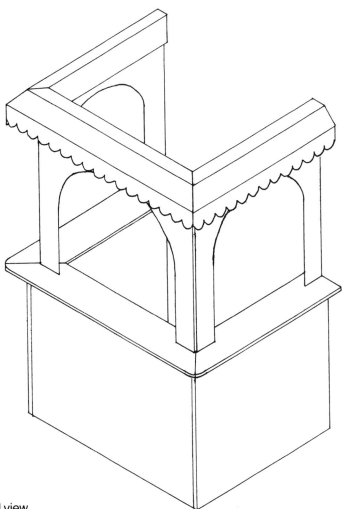

Fig 1 Assembled view

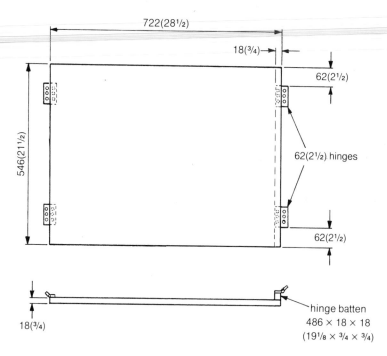

Fig 2 Base front
18(³/₄) thick

722(28½)

18(³/₄)

546(21½)

62(2½)

62(2½) hinges

62(2½)

18(³/₄)

hinge batten
486 × 18 × 18
(19¹/₈ × ³/₄ × ³/₄)

Leftover rolls of vinyl wallpaper can be used to paint backdrops, and this is where the children can help out. If only one backdrop is going to be used, this can easily be attached across the back opening using adhesive tape.

If more than one backdrop is required for a play, they can be attached in order of appearance around a broom handle (750mm, 29½in) long, which in turn is secured to the top of the side sunblinds by means of conduit pipe clips. The painted backdrops can now be flipped over when required. It may be necessary to attach large paper clips to the bottom of the backdrops to prevent them from curling.

To give an extra flare to the theatre, angle-poise torches (lanterns) can be fixed to the top inside corners as spot lights. Coloured cellophane can be taped over the torches to give different effects.

The possibilities are endless and I will leave any more ideas to the more adventurous.

When play has finished, or mum wants her lounge back, the shop/theatre can easily be dismantled and folded away.

1 Start by cutting out the three base sides (see Fig 2 and cutting list). Then screw and glue the 490×18×18mm (19¹/₄×³/₄×³/₄in) hinge batten to one side of the base front. This will enable the base walls to fold away.

2 Now screw four 65mm (2½in) hinges in position, drilling pilot holes first. Sand all rough edges smooth, small splinters can find their way into small fingers.

3 Mark and cut out counter assemblies (Figs 3 and 4), working on one counter at a time. Do not cut the 89mm (3½in) radii until all counters are in position on the base wall. Also do not shape the battens underneath the counters until they are glued in position.

4 Mark the positions of the battens on the underside of the counter, and glue the battens in position, using cramps until glue has dried. To make sure the battens

*Doll's Pram (see page 44) and Shop/Puppet Theatre (see page 49)*

50

Fig 3 Front counter

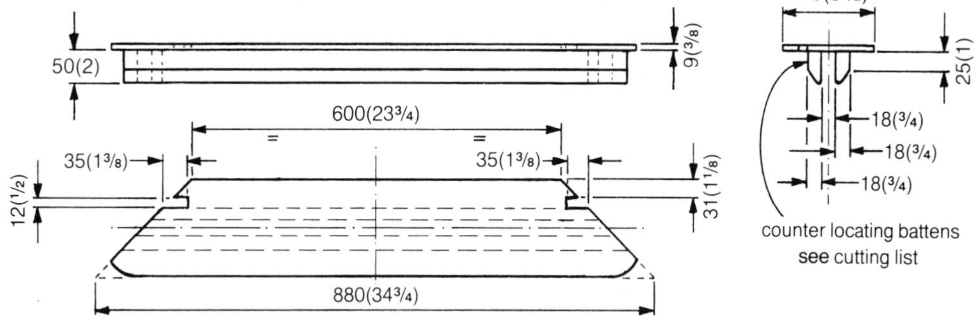

140(5½)
50(2)
9(⅜)
25(1)
600(23¾)
18(¾)
35(1⅜)
35(1⅜)
18(¾)
12(½)
18(¾)
31(1⅛)
counter locating battens
see cutting list
880(34¾)


Fig 4 Side counter
make one for each side

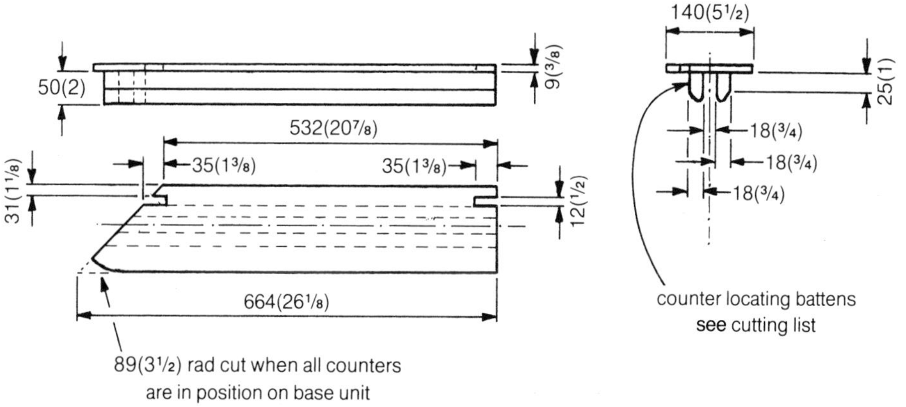

140(5½)
50(2)
9(⅜)
25(1)
532(20⅞)
18(¾)
31(1⅛)
35(1⅜)
35(1⅜)
18(¾)
12(½)
18(¾)
664(26⅛)
counter locating battens
see cutting list
89(3½) rad cut when all counters
are in position on base unit


**Base sides** make two 603 × 546 × 18(23¾ × 21½ × ¾)

stay parallel use a piece of 18mm (¾in) plywood as a spacer, making sure it does not come into contact with any glue that may seep into the channel.

5 Shape the under counter battens, rounding off the lower edges to ease location over the base walls. The inside of the channel can be greased with candle wax, to ease fitting and removal.

6 All counters are made in the same way. When they are finished, slot them over the base walls, mark and cut the 89mm (3½in) radii.

*Pony Stable (see page 101) and Farmyard (see page 17)*

7 The arch walls (Figs 5 and 6) are next to be made and the large radii are marked out with the help of a scrap piece of wood which is longer than 267mm (10½in). Drive a nail through one end of this scrap wood which will act as the point of our home-made compass. Drill two holes 267mm (10½in) and 203mm (8in) away from the nail point. These holes are determined by the size of pencil you are going to use, making sure the pencil is a tight fit.

8 When the arches have been cut and sanded, pin and glue the 35×12mm (1⅜×½in) battens in position, joining them at the top with a 45° angle. Plane the outside edges to 45° (vertical battens only) and pin and glue the 23×23mm (⅞×⅞in) square battens in position. These 23×23mm ⅞×⅞in) battens are only for the front arch wall.

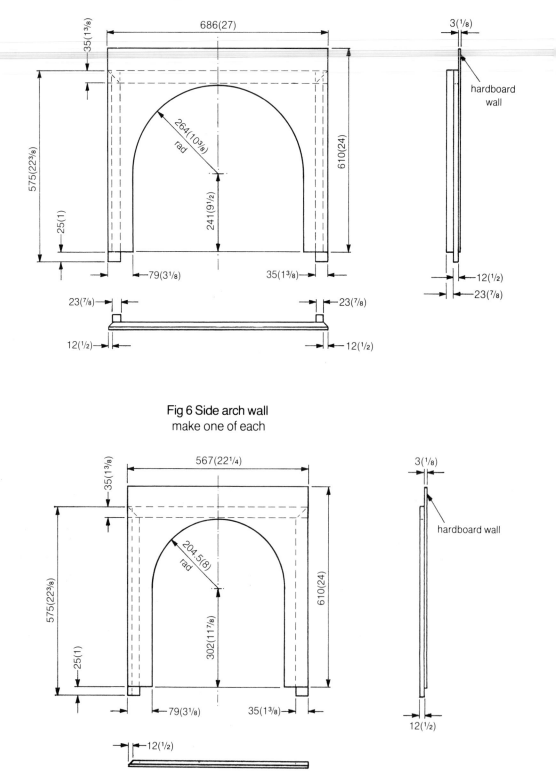

## Fig 5 Front arch wall

686(27)

35(1³/₈)

3(¹/₈)

hardboard wall

575(22³/₈)

610(24)

264(10³/₈) rad

241(9¹/₂)

25(1)

79(3¹/₈)

35(1³/₈)

12(¹/₂)

23(⁷/₈)

23(⁷/₈)

23(⁷/₈)

12(¹/₂)

12(¹/₂)

12(¹/₂)

## Fig 6 Side arch wall
### make one of each

567(22¹/₄)

35(1³/₈)

3(¹/₈)

hardboard wall

575(22³/₈)

610(24)

204.5(8) rad

302(11⁷/₈)

25(1)

79(3¹/₈)

35(1³/₈)

12(¹/₂)

12(¹/₂)

Fig 7 Sun blind formers
make twelve, 6(¼) thick

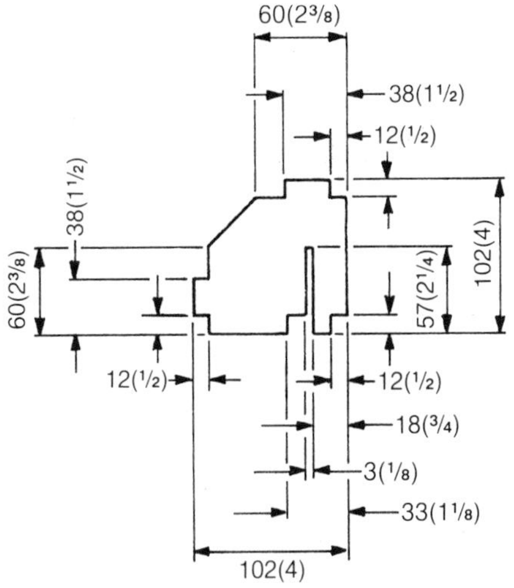
60(2⅜)
38(1½)
12(½)
102(4)
60(2⅜)
38(1½)
57(2¼)
12(½)
12(½)
18(¾)
3(⅛)
33(1⅛)
102(4)

Fig 8 Assembly positions of sunblind
stringers and panels

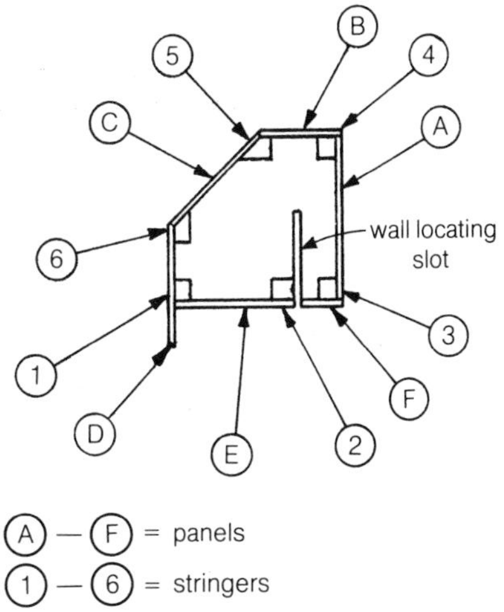
5
B
4
C
A
wall locating slot
6
3
1
F
D
E
2
A — F = panels
1 — 6 = stringers

9 Slot the arch walls through the counters and screw together.
10 Make 12 sunblind formers (Fig 7) and cut the stringers to length, marking them for ease of reference later.
11 It will be seen from the drawings that sunblind panels are all lettered and the stringers are all numbered (Fig 8).
12 When assembling the front sunblind (Fig 9) all measurements are taken from the centre.
13 When assembling the side sunblinds (Fig 10) all measurements are taken from the end. All panels overlap the stop end panel with the exception of panels E and F.
14 To add strength to the sunblind assemblies, cut short lengths of wood and glue them in the corners where the stringers meet the formers.
15 *Painting* Make sure you use lead-free paints. The colour scheme is up to you, but *do not* paint the areas where the counters slot onto the base walls, or the area where the sunblinds slot onto the arch walls.
16 The till shelf (Fig 11) will stop your child's till from crashing to the ground every time he/she opens it, but dimensions X and Y will depend on the size of till that is used.

**Cutting list**

| | | | |
|---|---|---|---|
| Base front (Fig 2) | 1 off | 722×546×18mm (28½×21½×¾in) | Plywood |
| Hinge batten (Fig 2) | 1 off | 486×18×18mm (19⅛×¾×¾in) | Wood |
| Base sides (Fig 2) | 2 off | 603×546×18mm (23¾×21½×¾in) | Plywood |
| Front counter (Fig 3) | 1 off | 880×140×9mm (34¾×5½×⅜in) | Plywood |
| Counter locating battens | 1 off | 800×50×18mm (31½×2×¾in) | Wood |
| (Fig 4) | 1 off | 724×50×18mm (28½×2×¾in) | Wood |
| Side counters (Fig 4) | 2 off | 664×140×9mm (26⅛×5½×⅜in) | Plywood |
| Counter locating battens (Fig 4) | 2 off | 621×50×18mm (24½×2×¾in) | Wood |
| | 2 off | 585×50×18mm (23×2×¾in) | Wood |
| Front arch wall (Fig 3) | 1 off | 686×610×3mm (27×24×⅛in) | Hardboard |
| Battens | 1 off | 688×35×12mm (27×1⅜×½in) | Wood |
| | 2 off | 575×35×12mm (22⅜×1⅜×½in) | Wood |
| | 2 off | 550×23×23mm (21⅜×⅞×⅞in) | Wood |

# Fig 9 Front sun blind
## Assembly of formers and stringers

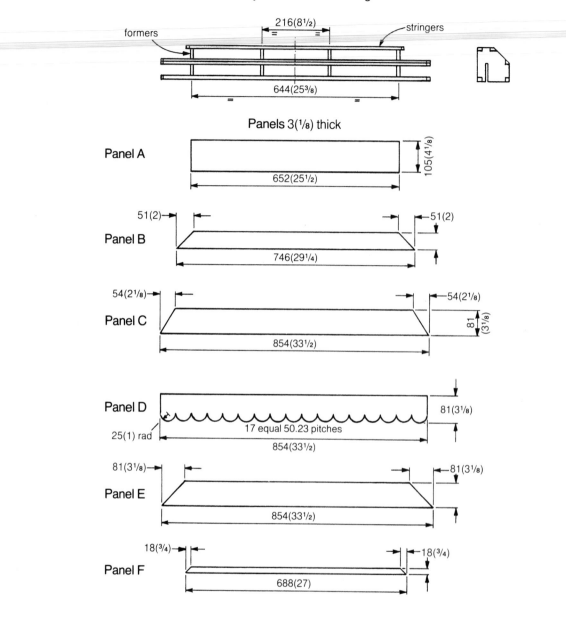

formers

216(8½)

stringers

644(25³⁄₈)

### Panels 3(⅛) thick

Panel A

652(25½)

105(4⅛)

Panel B

51(2)

51(2)

746(29¼)

Panel C

54(2⅛)

54(2⅛)

81 (3⅛)

854(33½)

Panel D

25(1) rad

17 equal 50.23 pitches

81(3⅛)

854(33½)

Panel E

81(3⅛)

81(3⅛)

854(33½)

Panel F

18(¾)

18(¾)

688(27)

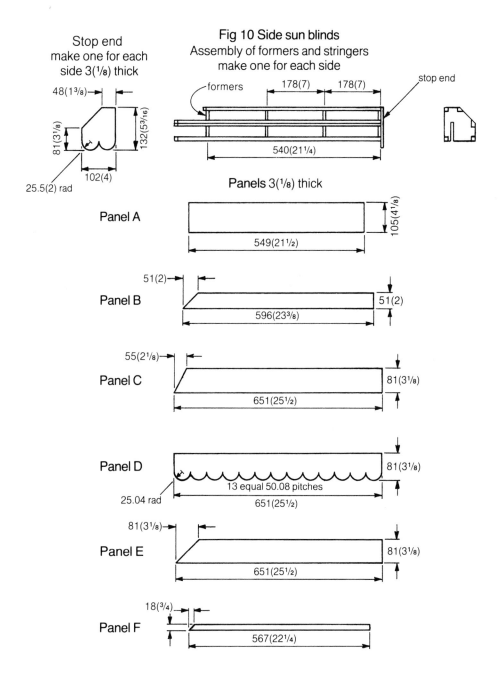

Stop end
make one for each
side 3(¹/₈) thick

48(1³/₈)

81(3¹/₈)

132(5³/₁₆)

102(4)

25.5(2) rad

## Fig 10 Side sun blinds
Assembly of formers and stringers
make one for each side

formers

178(7)   178(7)

stop end

540(21¹/₄)

## Panels 3(¹/₈) thick

Panel A

105(4¹/₈)

549(21¹/₂)

Panel B

51(2)

51(2)

596(23³/₈)

Panel C

55(2¹/₈)

81(3¹/₈)

651(25¹/₂)

Panel D

81(3¹/₈)

13 equal 50.08 pitches

25.04 rad

651(25¹/₂)

Panel E

81(3¹/₈)

81(3¹/₈)

651(25¹/₂)

Panel F

18(³/₄)

567(22¹/₄)

| | | | |
|---|---|---|---|
| Side arch walls (Fig 6) | 2 off | 567×610×3mm (22¼×24×⅛in) | Hardboard |
| | 4 off | 575×35×12mm (22⅜×1⅜×½in) | Wood |
| | 2 off | 567×35×12mm (22¼×1⅜×½in) | Wood |
| Sun blind formers (Fig 7) | 12 off | 102×102×6mm (4×4×¼in) | Plywood |
| Front sun blind stringers (Fig 9) 1 | 1 off | 854×12×12mm (33½×½×½in) | Wood |
| 2 | 1 off | 716×12×12mm (28¼×½×½in) | Wood |
| 3 and 4 | 1 off | 676×12×12mm (26½×½×½in) | Wood |
| 5 | 1 off | 764×12×22mm (30×½×⅞in) | Wood |
| 6 | 1 off | 854×12×22mm (33½×½×⅞in) | Wood |
| Front sun blind panels (Fig 9)   A | 1 off | 652×105×3mm (25½×4⅛×⅛in) | Hardboard |
| B | 1 off | 746×51×3mm (29¼×2×⅛in) | Hardboard |
| C, D and E | 1 off | 854×81×3mm (33½×3⅛×⅛in) | Hardboard |
| F | 1 off | 688×18×3mm (27×¾×⅛in) | Hardboard |
| Side sun blind stringers (Fig 10) 1 | 2 off | 651×12×12mm (25½×½×½in) | Wood |
| 2 | 2 off | 582×12×12mm (22⅞×½×½in) | Wood |
| Side sun blind stringers 3 & 4 | 2 off | 561×12×12mm (22×½×½in) | Wood |
| 5 | 2 off | 554×12×22mm (21¾×½×⅞in) | Wood |
| 6 | 2 off | 651×12×22mm (25½×½×⅞in) | Wood |
| Side sun blind panels (Fig 10)  A | 2 off | 549×105×3mm (21½×4⅛×⅛in) | Hardboard |
| B | 2 off | 596×51×3mm (23⅜×2×⅛in) | Hardboard |
| C, D and E | 2 off | 651×81×3mm (25½×3⅛×⅛in) | Hardboard |
| F | 2 off | 567×18×3mm (22¼×¾×⅛in) | Hardboard |
| Side sun blind stop ends | 2 off | 102×132×3mm (4×5³/₁₆×⅛in) | Hardboard |

*Ancillaries*

| | | |
|---|---|---|
| Hinges | 4 off | 62mm (2½in) |
| Till shelf | | *See* Fig 11 |

Fig 11 Assembled till shelf

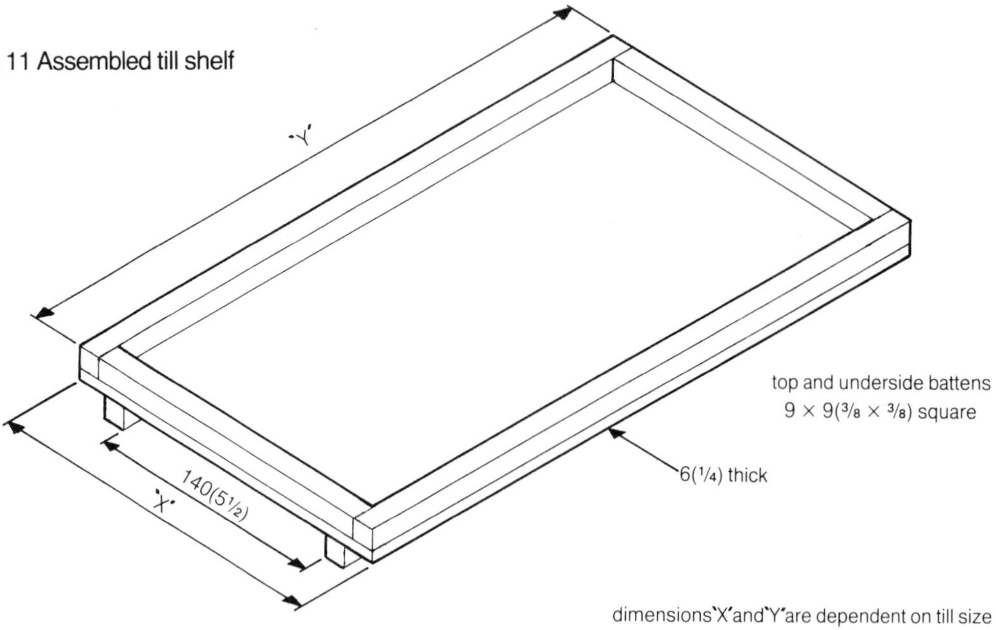

top and underside battens
9 × 9(³/₈ × ³/₈) square

6(¼) thick

140(5½)

'X'   'Y'

dimensions 'X' and 'Y' are dependent on till size

# CASTLE

*(shown in colour on page 69)*

Children have been playing with toy castles ever since the real castles were first built centuries ago.

Until recently castles have mainly been a boy's toy and only used with knights in armour. But since the arrival of a larger-than-life cartoon character and all his friends, this has changed.

Now girls can use this castle to play with their favourite characters too and maybe play alongside the boys, each with their own role.

My original intention with this project was to hinge the two units together, but on the direction of my chief tester (my son) they were left as two separate units to make either one large castle or two separate smaller castles. 'Goodies' versus 'baddies'.

There is quite a lot of repetitive work involved in making this castle, and wherever possible it is helpful to make one good pattern of the parts required and use this pattern to mark out other parts of the same type.

1 Start by marking and cutting out one front wall (Fig 1). Remove the castellations by cutting vertically with a tenon saw and removing the centre with a coping saw. Make sure that the castellations to be removed are clearly marked to avoid cutting out the wrong area.

2 Remove the windows and door archway (*see* Methods and materials, page 9).

3 When all rough edges of the first front wall have been sanded, it is then possible to use this wall as a pattern to mark out the second wall.

4 Although there are four different types of tower wall (Figs 2, 3, 4 and 5), they all have the same outside dimensions. These can now be marked and cut out. Use the first tower wall made as a pattern to mark out the others. Label each wall as it is made so that too many of the same type are not made.

5 The tower floors and portcullis (Figs 6-9)

are next to be made. Portcullis openings are made as described in Methods and materials (page 9, window and door openings).

6 Before the towers can be assembled as whole units, the corner blocks, floor support blocks and portcullis guide blocks have to be glued into position. Also at this stage, glue one bottom floor to each wall B, and one bottom floor to two walls C.

7 When fitting portcullis guide blocks, ensure there is free movement for the portcullis to slide.

8 Assemble towers one at a time, and then join them to the front walls as shown in Fig 10. The $364 \times 12 \times 12$mm ($14\frac{1}{4} \times \frac{1}{2} \times \frac{1}{2}$) walkway support block is fitted between towers A and B after they have been joined to the front wall.

9 Cut out the two bases (Fig 11). Place the assembled towers and front walls on to the bases. Mark their outline and then drill and countersink fixing holes in the base.

10 The winch handle assembly (Figs 12 and 16) is the next thing to make and you will find it easier to make the cogs (Fig 13) if they are marked out completely before cutting them to their finished size.

Both the cogs and the limit stops (Fig 14) must be a slide fit on the winch drum so that they can be fitted after the towers have been assembled. This is mainly to make painting easier.

When fitted to its axle, the latch (Fig 15) must also be a slide fit so that it will engage in the teeth of the cog automatically. The axle must be a tight fit through the 3mm ($\frac{1}{8}$in) dia holes at the top of each tower. Both cog and latch should be made from hardwood.

11 Smooth off all edges and paint.

12 For dragon pattern *see* Scaling Tower (page 72).

13 To make up step formers follow Fig 17.

14 To give the impression that the castles are made from stone blocks use a permanent marker which has a fine point to draw in the stonework.

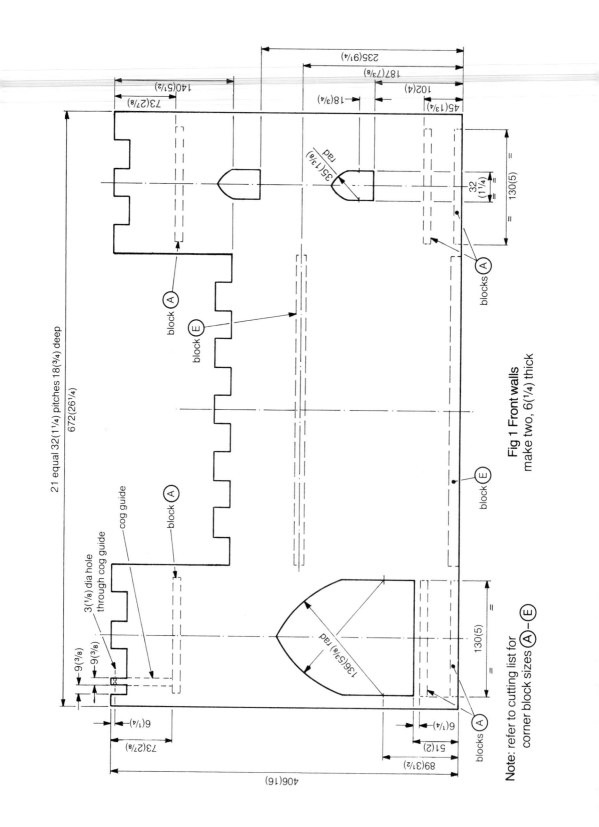

**Fig 1 Front walls**
make two, 6(¼) thick

Note: refer to cutting list for
corner block sizes Ⓐ – Ⓔ

21 equal 32(1¼) pitches 18(¾) deep
672(26¼)

3(⅛) dia hole
through cog guide

cog guide

block Ⓐ

block Ⓔ

block Ⓐ

block Ⓔ

blocks Ⓐ

blocks Ⓐ

136(5⅜) rad

35(1⅜) rad

140(5½)
73(27⁄8)
235(9¼)
187(7⅜)
102(4)
45(1¾)
18(¾)

32(1¼)

130(5)

130(5)

9(⅜)
9(⅜)
6(¼)
73(27⁄8)
406(16)

6(¼)
51(2)
89(3½)

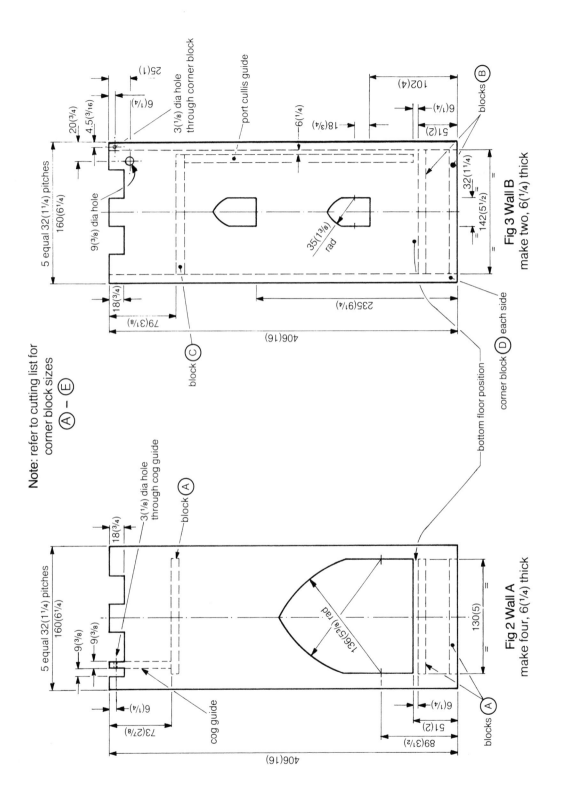

Note: refer to cutting list for corner block sizes Ⓐ – Ⓔ

**Fig 2 Wall A**
make four, 6(1/4) thick

cog guide

3(1/8) dia hole through cog guide

block Ⓐ

blocks Ⓐ

5 equal 32(1 1/4) pitches
160(6 1/4)

18(3/4)

9(3/8)

9(3/8)

6(1/4)

73(2 7/8)

406(16)

51(2)

89(3 1/2)

6(1/4)

130(5)

136(5 3/8) rad

**Fig 3 Wall B**
make two, 6(1/4) thick

block Ⓒ

port cullis guide

3(1/8) dia hole through corner block

9(3/8) dia hole

25(1)

6(1/4)

20(3/4)

4.5(3/16)

5 equal 32(1 1/4) pitches
160(6 1/4)

18(3/4)

79(3 1/8)

406(16)

235(9 1/4)

35(1 3/8) rad

6(1/4)

18(3/4)

51(2)

6(1/4)

102(4)

32(1 1/4)

142(5 1/2)

blocks Ⓑ

corner block Ⓓ each side

bottom floor position

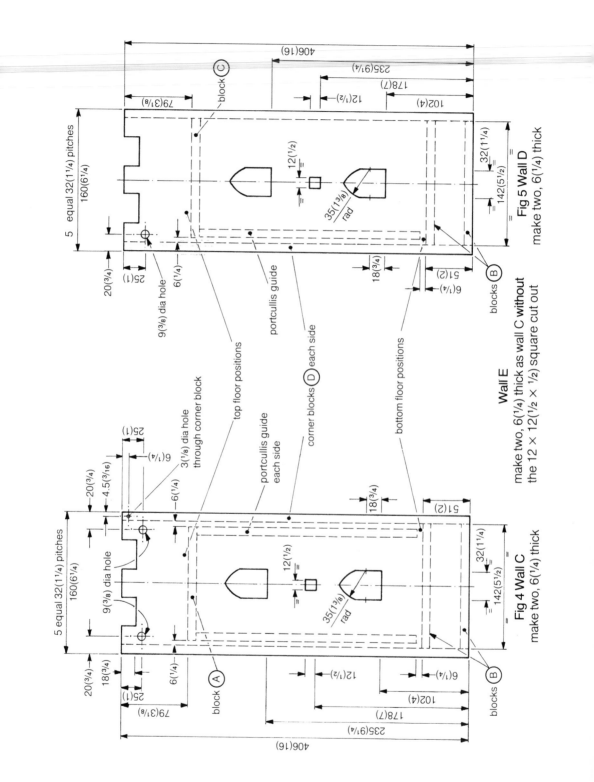

**Fig 4 Wall C**
make two, 6(1/4) thick

**Fig 5 Wall D**
make two, 6(1/4) thick

**Wall E**
make two, 6(1/4) thick as wall C without
the 12 × 12(1/2 × 1/2) square cut out

block A

blocks B

blocks B

block C

corner blocks D each side

3(1/8) dia hole
through corner block

9(3/8) dia hole

9(3/8) dia hole

top floor positions

portcullis guide
each side

portcullis guide

bottom floor positions

5 equal 32(1 1/4) pitches
160(6 1/4)

5 equal 32(1 1/4) pitches
160(6 1/4)

406(16)

406(16)

235(9 1/4)

235(9 1/4)

178(7)

178(7)

102(4)

102(4)

12(1/2)

12(1/2)

12(1/2)

12(1/2)

35(1 3/8)
rad

35(1 3/8)
rad

142(5 1/2)

142(5 1/2)

32(1 1/4)

32(1 1/4)

51(2)

51(2)

18(3/4)

18(3/4)

6(1/4)

6(1/4)

6(1/4)

6(1/4)

25(1)

25(1)

25(1)

20(3/4)

20(3/4)

20(3/4)

18(3/4)

4.5(3/16)

79(3 1/8)

79(3 1/8)

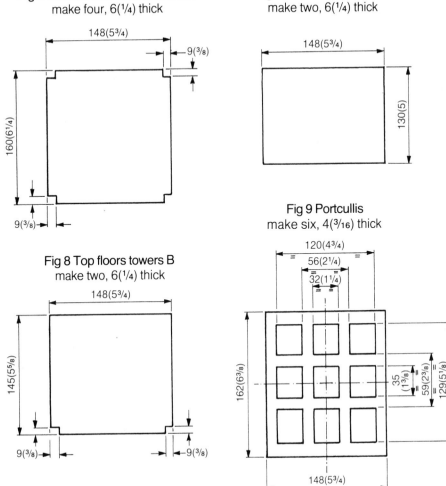

Fig 6 Bottom floor towers A and B
make four, 6(¼) thick

148(5¾)

9(³/₈)

160(6¼)

9(³/₈)

Fig 7 Top floors towers A
make two, 6(¼) thick

148(5¾)

130(5)

Fig 9 Portcullis
make six, 4(³/₁₆) thick

120(4¾)
56(2¼)
32(1¼)

162(6³/₈)

35 (1³/₈)
59(2³/₈)
129(5¹/₈)

148(5¾)

Fig 8 Top floors towers B
make two, 6(¼) thick

148(5¾)

145(5⁵/₈)

9(³/₈)

9(³/₈)

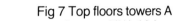

63

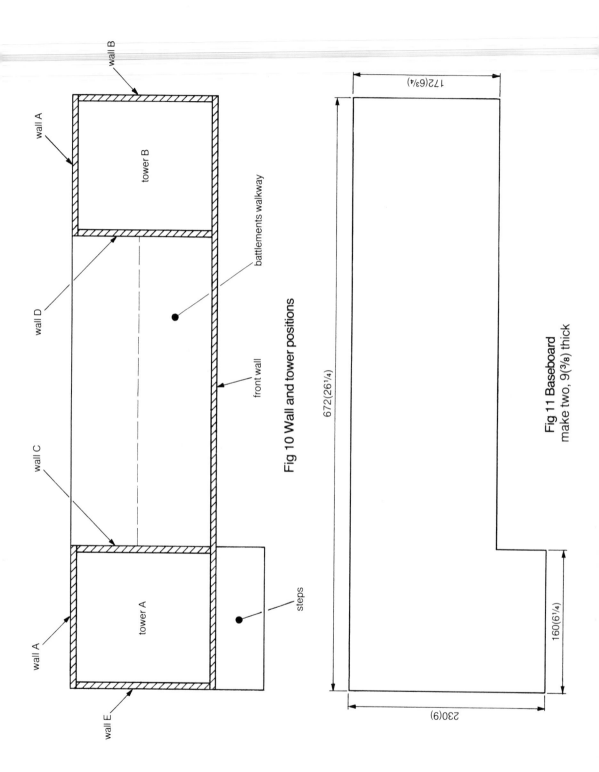

wall B

wall A

tower B

wall D

wall C

wall A

tower A

wall E

battlements walkway

front wall

steps

**Fig 10 Wall and tower positions**

672(26¼)

172(6¾)

160(6¼)

230(9)

**Fig 11 Baseboard**
make two, 9(3/8) thick

## Fig 12 Winch handle
make six, 9(³⁄₈) thick

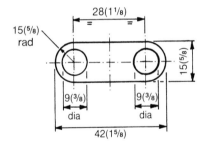

28(1¹⁄₈)

15(⁵⁄₈) rad

15(⁵⁄₈)

9(³⁄₈) dia

9(³⁄₈) dia

42(1⁵⁄₈)

## Fig 13 Cog
make six, 9(³⁄₈)thick

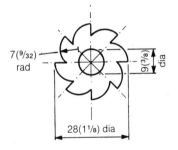

7(⁹⁄₃₂) rad

9(³⁄₈) dia

28(1¹⁄₈) dia

## Fig 14 Winch drum limit stop
make twelve, 6(¹⁄₄) thick

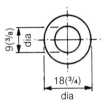

9(³⁄₈) dia

18(³⁄₄) dia

## Fig 15 Latch
make six, 9(³⁄₈) thick

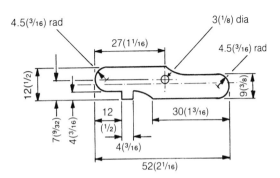

4.5(³⁄₁₆) rad

27(1¹⁄₁₆)

3(¹⁄₈) dia

4.5(³⁄₁₆) rad

9(³⁄₈)

12(¹⁄₂)

7(⁹⁄₃₂)

4(³⁄₁₆)

12 (¹⁄₂)

30(1³⁄₁₆)

4(³⁄₁₆)

52(2¹⁄₁₆)

## Fig 16 Winch handle assembly

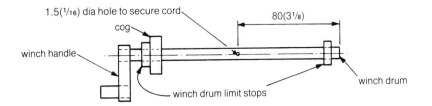

1.5(¹⁄₁₆) dia hole to secure cord

cog

winch handle

80(3¹⁄₈)

winch drum limit stops

winch drum

Do not glue any of these parts together until they are in position in the towers. When glueing parts to winch drum, leave as little sideways movement as possible without fouling the side walls. Free movement is essential

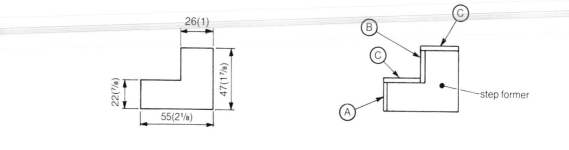

Fig 17 Step formers
make six, 6(¼) thick

assembled side view showing
step tread positions

26(1)

22(⅞)

47(1⅞)

55(2⅛)

—step former

## Cutting list for two units

| | | | | |
|---|---|---|---|---|
| Front walls (Fig 1) | 2 off | 406×672×6mm (16×26¼×¼in) | | Plywood |
| Tower walls A,B,C,D,E (Figs 2, 3, 4 and 5) | 12 off | 406×160×6mm (16×6¼×¼in) | | Plywood |
| Top floor tower B (Fig 8) | 2 off | 148×145×6mm (5¾×5⅝×¼in) | | Plywood |
| Top floor tower A (Fig 7) | 2 off | 148×130×6mm (5¾×5×¼in) | | Plywood |
| Bottom floor tower A, B (Fig 6) | 4 off | 148×160×6mm (5¾×6¼×¼in) | | Plywood |
| Baseboard (Fig 11) | 2 off | 672×230×9mm (26¼×9×⅜in) | | Plywood |
| Battlement walkway (Fig 10) | 2 off | 352×86×3mm (13¾×3⅜×⅛in) | | Hardboard |
| | 2 off | 364×12×12mm (14¼×½×½in) | | Wood |
| Corner & floor | 1 | 28 off | 130×9×9mm (5×⅜×⅜in) | Wood |
| support blocks | 2 | 12 off | 142×9×9mm (5½×⅜×⅜in) | Wood |
| | 3 | 4 off | 136×9×9mm (5¼×⅜×⅜in) | Wood |
| | 4 | 16 off | 406×9×9mm (16×⅜×⅜in) | Wood |
| | 5 | 4 off | 352×12×12mm (13¾×½×½in) | Wood |
| Portcullis guides | 12 off | 268×9×9mm (10½×⅜×⅜in) | | Wood |
| Portcullis (Fig 9) | 6 off | 16×148×4mm (6⅜×5¾×3/16) | | Plywood |
| Step formers (Fig 17) | 6 off | 55×35×6mm (2⅛×1⅜×¼in) | | Plywood |
| Step treads A | 2 off | 22×160×3mm (⅞×6¼×⅛in) | | Plywood |
| B | 2 off | 25×160×3mm (1×6¼×⅛in) | | Plywood |
| C | 4 off | 29×160×9mm (1⅛×6¼×⅛in) | | Plywood |
| Cogs (Fig 13) | 6 off | 29mm(1⅛in)dia×9mm(⅜in) thick | | Hardwood |
| Cog guides | 6 off | 73×9×9mm (2⅞×⅜×⅜in) | | Wood |
| Winch drums (Fig 14) | 6 off | 172mm(6¾in)×9mm(⅜in)dia dowel | | |
| Winch handles (Fig 12) | 6 off | 42×15×9mm (1⅝×⅝×⅜in) | | Hardwood |
| | 6 off | 29×15×9mm (1⅛×⅝×⅜in) | | Hardwood |
| Winch drum limit stop (Fig 14) | 12 off | 18mm(¾in)dia×6mm(¼in) thick dowel | | |
| Latches (Fig 15) | 6 off | 52×12×9mm (2 1/16×½×⅜in) | | Hardwood |
| Dragons | 2 off | *See* Siege Machines (page 73) | | |

*Ancillaries*

| | | |
|---|---|---|
| Latch axles | 6 off | 32mm(1¼in)long×3mm(⅛in)dia brass rod |
| Whipping twine | 6 off | 254mm(10in)lengths |

# SIEGE MACHINES AND LADDERS

*(shown in colour on page 69)*

These Siege Machines (scaling tower and catapult) and Ladders have been designed for use with the Castle (page 59) and the large figures that will be used with them.

They feature an operating arm on the catapult which can be loaded with ping-pong balls or tightly rolled up balls of tissue paper (nothing harder should be used). The scaling tower has a hinged boarding platform and a ladder.

Hardwood has been used for the construction of the ladders and chassis. This is because softwood has a tendency to tear when drilled.

## Scaling Tower

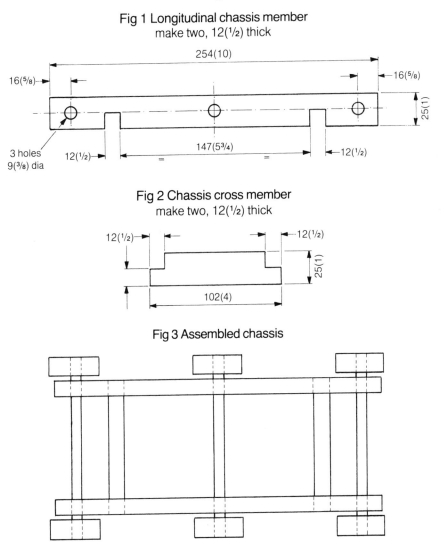

Fig 1 Longitudinal chassis member
make two, 12(½) thick

254(10)

16(⅝)

16(⅝)

25(1)

3 holes
9(⅜) dia

12(½)

147(5¾)

12(½)

Fig 2 Chassis cross member
make two, 12(½) thick

12(½)

12(½)

25(1)

102(4)

Fig 3 Assembled chassis

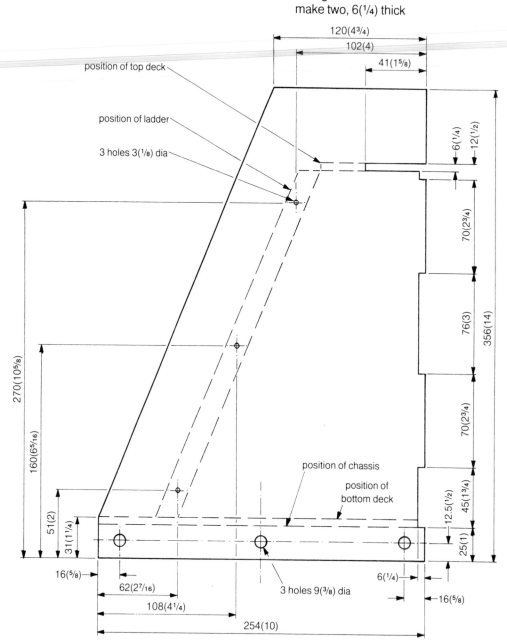

**Fig 4 Side wall**
make two, 6(¼) thick

position of top deck

position of ladder

3 holes 3(⅛) dia

120(4¾)

102(4)

41(1⅝)

6(¼)

12(½)

70(2¾)

76(3)

356(14)

70(2¾)

270(10⅝)

160(6⁵/₁₆)

position of chassis

position of
bottom deck

12.5(½)

45(1¾)

25(1)

51(2)

31(1¼)

16(⅝)

62(2⁷/₁₆)

108(4¼)

254(10)

3 holes 9(⅜) dia

6(¼)

16(⅝)

*Castle (see page 59) and Siege Machines
and Ladders (see page 67)*

## Fig 5 Front wall
### 6(¼) thick

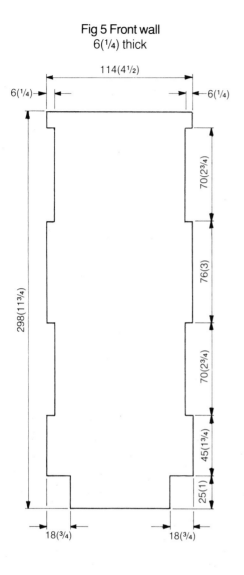

114(4½)

6(¼)

6(¼)

70(2¾)

76(3)

70(2¾)

45(1¾)

25(1)

298(11¾)

18(¾)

18(¾)

## Fig 6 Top deck
### 6(¼) thick

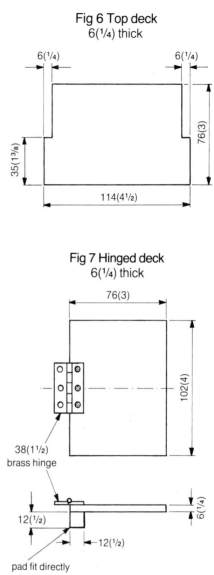

6(¼)

6(¼)

35(1⅜)

76(3)

114(4½)

## Fig 7 Hinged deck
### 6(¼) thick

76(3)

102(4)

38(1½)
brass hinge

12(½)

12(½)

6(¼)

pad fit directly
underneath hinge

*Split Level Cooker (see page 76) and Play
House (see page 81)*

## Fig 8 Scaling tower ladder
make two sides, 9(³⁄₈) thick

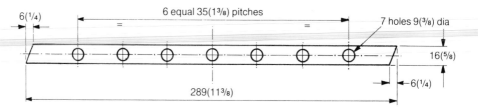

6(¼)

6 equal 35(1³⁄₈) pitches

=                  =

7 holes 9(³⁄₈) dia

16(⁵⁄₈)

6(¼)

289(11³⁄₈)

**Ladder rungs** make seven 102(4) long × 9(³⁄₈) dia dowel

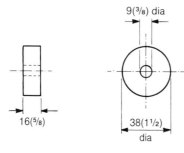

9(³⁄₈) dia

16(⁵⁄₈)

38(1½) dia

## Fig 9 Wheels
make six

## Fig 10 Dragon motif
1.5(¹⁄₁₆) thick birch plywood

9(³⁄₈) squares

1 The ladders can be made to any length using the drawings as a basis. For a natural finish use a light-oak wood stain applied with a brush and wiped over before dry with a clean soft cloth. The catapult is finished in teak oil applied with a soft cloth.
2 When drilling the axle and ladder rung holes, mark the centre of the hole on one side piece, clamp the two sides of the chassis or ladder together and drill through them both as one. Drilling holes this way means that you will have two identical parts and also save time marking and drilling.
3 Wheels for these models are made from 15mm (5/8in) thick hardwood using a hole cutter which has an inside blade dia of 66mm (15/8in). Use a file and glasspaper to remove rough edges.
4 The dragons for the side of the Scaling Tower and front of the Castle (page 59) are cut from 1.5mm (1/16in) thick birch plywood and stuck in place with a contact adhesive.

## Scaling tower cutting list

| | | | |
|---|---|---|---|
| Longitudinal chassis members (Fig 1) | 2 off | 254×25×12mm (10×1×1/2in) | Wood |
| Chassis cross member (Fig 2) | 2 off | 102×25×12mm (4×1×1/2in) | Wood |
| Side walls (Fig 4) | 2 off | 254×356×6mm (10×14×1/4in) | Plywood |
| Front wall (Fig 5) | 1 off | 298×114×6mm (113/4×41/2×1/4in) | Plywood |
| Bottom deck | 1 off | 245×102×6mm (93/4×4×1/4in) | Plywood |
| Top deck (Fig 6) | 1 off | 114×76×6mm (41/2×3×1/4in) | Plywood |
| Hinged deck (Fig 7) | 1 off | 76×102×6mm (3×4×1/4in) | Plywood |
| Pad (Fig 7) | 1 off | 38×12×6mm (11/2×1/2×1/4in) | Plywood |
| Corner block | 1 off | 102×12×12mm (4×1/2×1/2in) | Wood |
| Ladder sides (Fig 8) | 2 off | 289×16×12mm (115/8×5/8×1/2in) | Hardwood |
| Ladder rungs (Fig 8) | 7 off | 102mm(4in)long×9mm(3/8in)dia dowel | |
| Wheels (Fig 9) | 6 off | 38mm(11/2in)dia×16mm(5/8in) thick hardwood | |
| Axles | 3 off | 150mm(57/8in)long×9mm(3/8in)dia dowel | |

*Ancillaries*

| | | | |
|---|---|---|---|
| Hinge | 1 off | 38mm(11/2in) brass hinge | |
| Dragon (Fig 10) | made from | 1.5mm(1/16in) thick birch plywood | |

## Catapult cutting list

| | | | |
|---|---|---|---|
| Longitudinal chassis members (Fig 11) | 2 off | 254×25×12mm (10×1×1/2in) | Hardwood |
| Chassis cross member (Fig 12) | 2 off | 102×25×12mm (4×1×1/2in) | Hardwood |
| Uprights (Fig 13) | 2 off | 152×25×12mm (6×1×1/2in) | Hardwood |
| Top cross bar | 1 off | 102×25×12mm (4×1×1/2in) | Hardwood |
| Pivot dowel (Fig 15) | 1 off | 102mm(4in)long×9mm(3/8in)dia dowel | |
| Catapult arm stops (Fig 16) | 2 off | 12mm(1/2in)long×18mm(3/4in)dia dowel | |
| Catapult arm (Fig 15) | 1 off | 63mm(21/2in)long×9mm(3/8in)dia dowel | |
| | 1 off | 102mm(4in)long×9mm(3/8in)dia dowel | |
| | 1 off | 48×18×18mm (17/8×3/4×3/4in) | Hardwood |
| Spoon (Fig 15) | made from | 57×38×18mm (21/4×11/2×3/4in) | Hardwood |
| Axles | 3 off | 137mm(53/8in)long×9mm(3/8in)dia dowel | |
| Wheels | 6 off | 38mm(11/2in)dia×15mm(5/8in) thick hardwood | |

# Catapult

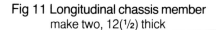

## Fig 11 Longitudinal chassis member
### make two, 12(½) thick

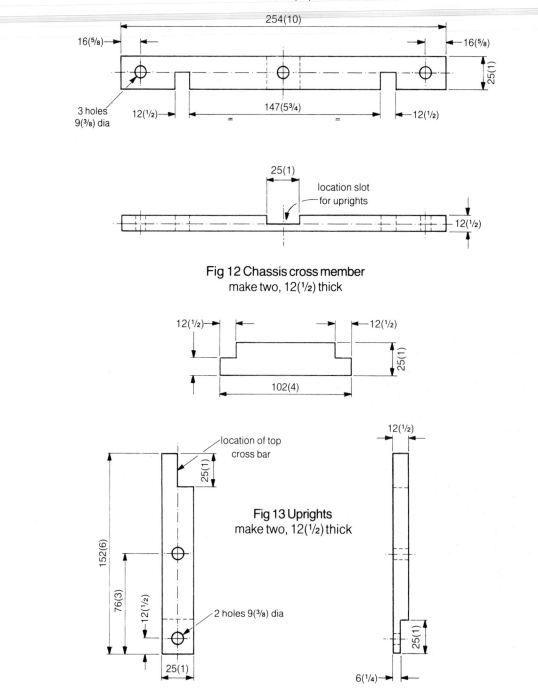

254(10)

16(⅝) — 16(⅝)

25(1)

3 holes
9(⅜) dia

12(½) — 12(½)

147(5¾)

=

=

25(1)

location slot
for uprights

12(½)

## Fig 12 Chassis cross member
### make two, 12(½) thick

12(½) — 12(½)

25(1)

102(4)

location of top
cross bar

25(1)

## Fig 13 Uprights
### make two, 12(½) thick

152(6)

76(3)

12(½)

2 holes 9(⅜) dia

25(1)

12(½)

25(1)

6(¼)

## Fig 14 Side view

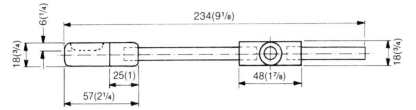

234(9⅛)

6(¼)

18(¾)

18(¾)

25(1)

48(1⅞)

57(2¼)

## Fig 15 Plan view

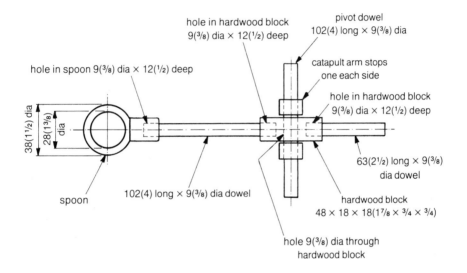

hole in hardwood block
9(⅜) dia × 12(½) deep

pivot dowel
102(4) long × 9(⅜) dia

hole in spoon 9(⅜) dia × 12(½) deep

catapult arm stops
one each side

hole in hardwood block
9(⅜) dia × 12(½) deep

38(1½) dia

28(1⅜) dia

63(2½) long × 9(⅜)
dia dowel

spoon

102(4) long × 9(⅜) dia dowel

hardwood block
48 × 18 × 18(1⅞ × ¾ × ¾)

hole 9(⅜) dia through
hardwood block

### Fig 16 Catapult arm stops
make two

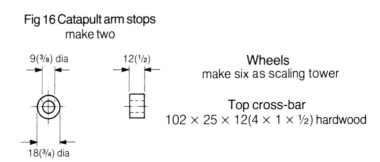

9(⅜) dia

12(½)

18(¾) dia

## Wheels
make six as scaling tower

## Top cross-bar
102 × 25 × 12(4 × 1 × ½) hardwood

# SPLIT LEVEL COOKER

*(shown in colour on page 70)*

Fig 1 Assembled view

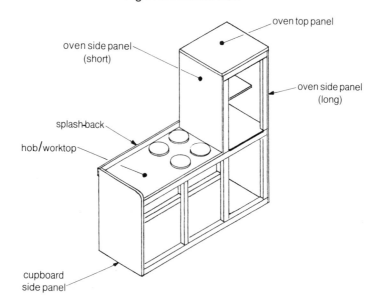

oven top panel

oven side panel
(short)

oven side panel
(long)

splash-back

hob/worktop

cupboard
side panel

The split-level cooker with its separate oven and hobs is an increasingly common sight these days in the modern kitchen.

Now the little cook of the family can also enjoy the advantages of split-level 'cooking' with this scaled-down version of the real thing.

Through the perspex oven door all manner of good things can be watched while they are 'cooking'. The space underneath the cupboards will provide a home for lots of secret things as well as pots and pans.

There is no bottom to the cupboards and this reduces the weight for carrying.

This project is designed so that it will fit neatly inside the play house (page 81) and add even more realism to a child's play.

1 Cut to length the rails that will make up the two main frames (Figs 1–6). Mark and cut out all main frame joints. Test assemble and clean out joints where needed before glueing.

Fig 2 Assembled front frame

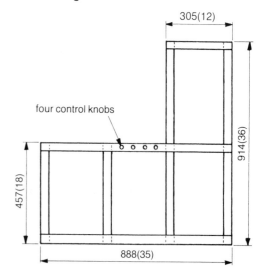

305(12)

four control knobs

914(36)

457(18)

888(35)

76

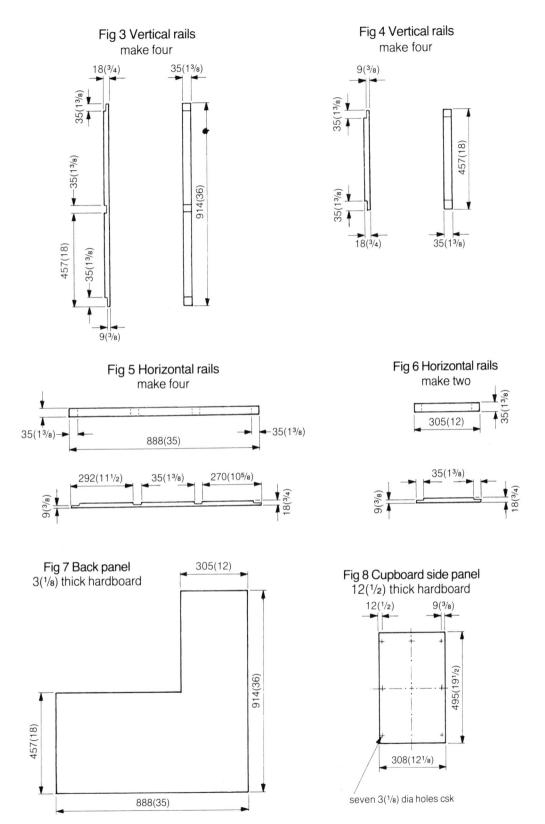

Fig 3 Vertical rails
make four

18(³/₄)　35(1³/₈)

35(1³/₈)

35(1³/₈)

914(36)

457(18)

35(1³/₈)

9(³/₈)

Fig 4 Vertical rails
make four

9(³/₈)

35(1³/₈)

457(18)

35(1³/₈)

18(³/₄)　35(1³/₈)

Fig 5 Horizontal rails
make four

35(1³/₈)　888(35)　35(1³/₈)

292(11¹/₂)　35(1³/₈)　270(10⁵/₈)

9(³/₈)　18(³/₄)

Fig 6 Horizontal rails
make two

305(12)　35(1³/₈)

35(1³/₈)

9(³/₈)　18(³/₄)

Fig 7 Back panel
3(¹/₈) thick hardboard

305(12)

914(36)

457(18)

888(35)

Fig 8 Cupboard side panel
12(¹/₂) thick hardboard

12(¹/₂)　9(³/₈)

495(19¹/₂)

308(12¹/₈)

seven 3(¹/₈) dia holes csk

77

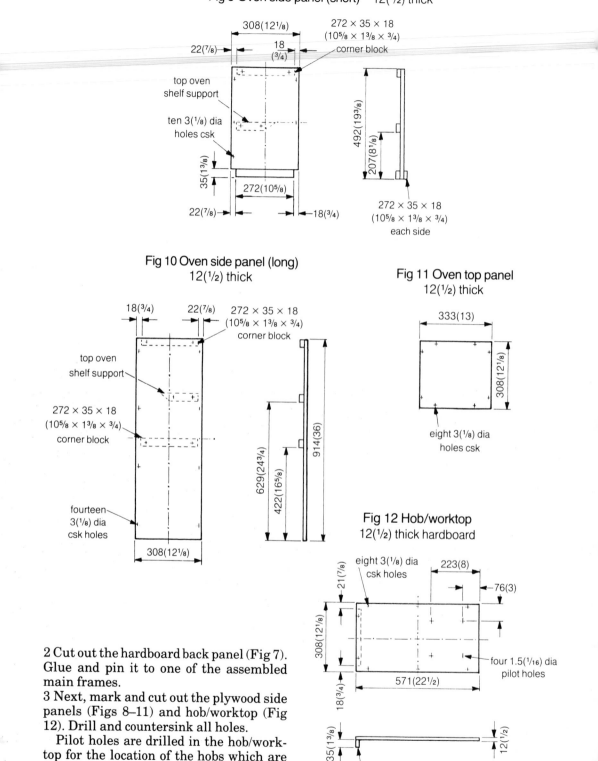

Fig 9 Oven side panel (short)   12(½) thick

308(12⅛)

272 × 35 × 18
(10⅝ × 1⅜ × ¾)
corner block

22(⅞)

18
(¾)

top oven
shelf support

ten 3(⅛) dia
holes csk

35(1⅜)

272(10⅝)

22(⅞)

18(¾)

492(19⅜)

207(8⅛)

272 × 35 × 18
(10⅝ × 1⅜ × ¾)
each side

Fig 10 Oven side panel (long)
12(½) thick

18(¾)

22(⅞)

272 × 35 × 18
(10⅝ × 1⅜ × ¾)
corner block

top oven
shelf support

272 × 35 × 18
(10⅝ × 1⅜ × ¾)
corner block

fourteen
3(⅛) dia
csk holes

308(12⅛)

914(36)

629(24¾)

422(16⅝)

Fig 11 Oven top panel
12(½) thick

333(13)

308(12⅛)

eight 3(⅛) dia
holes csk

Fig 12 Hob/worktop
12(½) thick hardboard

eight 3(⅛) dia
csk holes

223(8)

76(3)

21(⅞)

308(12⅛)

18(¾)

35(1⅜)

571(22½)

four 1.5(1/16) dia
pilot holes

12(½)

corner block

2 Cut out the hardboard back panel (Fig 7).
Glue and pin it to one of the assembled
main frames.

3 Next, mark and cut out the plywood side
panels (Figs 8–11) and hob/worktop (Fig
12). Drill and countersink all holes.

Pilot holes are drilled in the hob/work-
top for the location of the hobs which are
screwed in position after painting.

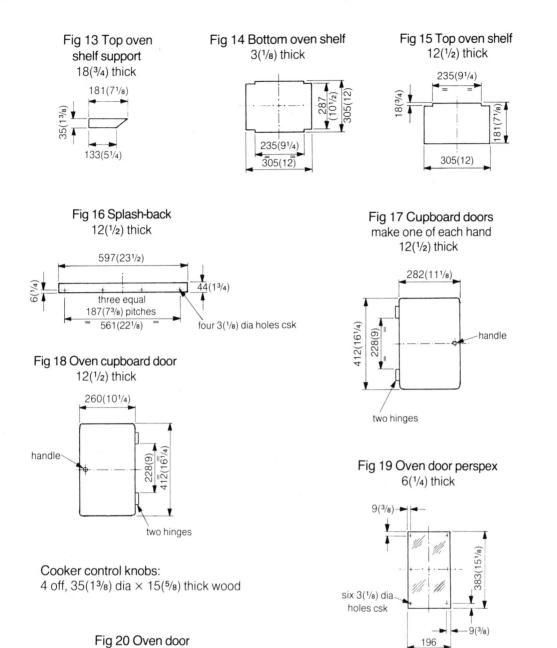

Fig 13 Top oven
shelf support
18(¾) thick

181(7⅛)

35(1⅜)

133(5¼)

Fig 14 Bottom oven shelf
3(⅛) thick

287
(10½)

305(12)

235(9¼)

305(12)

Fig 15 Top oven shelf
12(½) thick

235(9¼)

18(¾)

181(7⅛)

305(12)

Fig 16 Splash-back
12(½) thick

597(23½)

6(¼)

44(1¾)

three equal
187(7⅜) pitches

561(22⅛)

four 3(⅛) dia holes csk

Fig 17 Cupboard doors
make one of each hand
12(½) thick

282(11⅛)

412(16¼)

228(9)

handle

two hinges

Fig 18 Oven cupboard door
12(½) thick

260(10¼)

handle

228(9)

412(16¼)

two hinges

Fig 19 Oven door perspex
6(¼) thick

9(⅜)

383(15⅛)

six 3(⅛) dia
holes csk

9(⅜)

196
(7¾)

Cooker control knobs:
4 off, 35(1⅜) dia × 15(⅝) thick wood

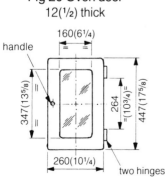

Fig 20 Oven door
12(½) thick

160(6¼)

handle

347(13⅝)

264
=(10¾)=

447(17⅝)

260(10¼)

two hinges

4 Glue and screw all corner blocks and shelf supports to their respective side panels.

5 Lay the frame, which has the hardboard panel fixed to it, on its back on a flat surface. Then glue and screw the plywood side panels to this frame.

6 Stand the whole assembly upright and glue and screw the front frame in position.

7 Pin and glue the 3mm (⅛in) thick bottom oven shelf (Fig 14) in position. Then screw and glue the top oven shelf (Fig 15), oven top panel (Fig 11) and splash-back (Fig 16) in position.

8 Mark and cut out the cupboard doors (Figs 17 and 18). Also mark and cut out the perspex for the oven door (Figs 19 and 20), drill and countersink the fixing holes.

Do not screw the perspex in place until all of the painting has been completed.

**Note** the cupboard and oven doors overlap the frames by 12mm (½in) each side.

9 Paint as required.

10 Screw hinges, magnetic catches and door handles to the doors and fit them in place on the finished unit.

Magnetic door catches will be easier for children to operate than other types of door catches.

11 Screw the hobs to the worktop using the pilot holes already drilled.

## Cutting list

| | | | |
|---|---|---|---|
| Main frame vertical | | | |
| rails (Fig 3) | 4 off | 914×35×18mm (36×1⅜×¾in) | Wood |
| (Fig 4) | 4 off | 457×35×18mm (18×1⅜×¾in) | Wood |
| horizontal rails | | | |
| (Fig 5) | 4 off | 888×35×18mm (35×1⅜×¾in) | Wood |
| (Fig 6) | 2 off | 305×35×18mm (12×1⅜×¾in) | Wood |
| Back panel (Fig 7) | 1 off | 888×914×3mm (35×36×⅛in) | Hardboard |
| Cupboard side panel | | | |
| (Fig 8) | 1 off | 308×495×12mm (12⅛×19½×½in) | Plywood |
| Hob/worktop (Fig 12) | 1 off | 308×571×12mm (12⅛×22½×½in) | Plywood |
| corner block | 1 off | 269×35×18mm (10½×1⅜×¾in) | Wood |
| hobs | 4 off | 100mm(4in)dia×6mm(¼in)thick | Plywood |
| Oven side panel | | | |
| (short) (Fig 9) | 1 off | 308×492×12mm (12⅛×19⅜×½in) | Plywood |
| corner block/shelf | | | |
| supports | 3 off | 269×35×18mm (10½×1⅜×¾in) | Wood |
| shelf support (Fig 13) | 1 off | 181×35×18mm (7⅛×1⅜×¾in) | Wood |
| Oven side panel | | | |
| (long) (Fig 10) | 1 off | 914×308×12mm (36×12⅛×½in) | Plywood |
| corner block/shelf | | | |
| supports | 2 off | 269×35×18mm (10½×1⅜×¾in) | Wood |
| shelf support | 1 off | 181×35×18mm (7⅛×1⅜×¾in) | Wood |
| Bottom oven shelf | | | |
| (Fig 14) | 1 off | 305×305×3mm (12×12×⅛in) | Plywood |
| Top oven shelf (Fig 15) | 1 off | 305×181×12mm (12×7⅛×½in) | Plywood |
| Oven top panel (Fig 11) | 1 off | 333×308×12mm (13×12⅛×½in) | Plywood |
| Splash-back (Fig 16) | 1 off | 597×44×12mm (23½×1¾×½in) | Plywood |
| Cupboard doors (Fig 17) | 2 off | 412×282×12mm (16¼×11⅛×½in) | Plywood |
| Oven doors | | | |
| (Figs 19 and 20) | 1 off | 447×260×12mm (17⅝×10¼×½in) | Plywood |
| Oven cupboard door | | | |
| (Fig 18) | 1 off | 412×260×12mm (16¼×10¼×½in) | Plywood |
| | | | |
| *Ancillaries* | | | |
| | 1 off | 383×196×6mm (15⅛×7¾×¼in) | Perspex |
| | 8 off | 50mm (2in) long cabinet (crank) hinges | |
| | 4 off | Magnetic door catches | |
| | 4 off | Door knobs (small) | |
| Hob controls | 4 off | 35mm(1⅜in)dia×12mm(½in)thick | Plywood |

80

# PLAY HOUSE

*(shown in colour on page 70)*

This play house provides a sizeable area for children to play in, and with the top braces in position the structure is very rigid.

When not in use, or if rain suddenly stops play, it can easily be folded flat and stored.

There is plenty of room inside for the Split Level Cooker (page 76) which will add realism to a child's furtive imagination, and they will soon be 'cooking' their own meals.

1 Hardboard comes in sheets which measure 2240×1220mm (8ft×4ft) and one and a half sheets are required for this project. It may not be possible to buy half a sheet, and you will then have to buy two sheets. Cut them out as shown (Figs 1 and 2).

If a jigsaw is used, a fine toothed blade must be fitted.

2 Starting with the side walls, cut the 35×18mm (1⅜×¾in) wood pieces (Figs 3, 4, 5a, 5b) to length.

3 Because the rails overlap each other at various points, an equal amount of wood has to be removed from each rail at the point of overlap (ie ½ thickness) so that the rails will lay flat against the hardboard wall.

To do this, mark the position of the joint, and using a tenon saw cut the outside edges of the joint. Now make an extra cut in the centre of the joint. This will ease the removal of the waste wood.

Using a sharp chisel start to remove the waste wood. Do not attempt to remove all the waste from one side, but take some from each side until it is possible to clean the joint right through. Trying to do it all in one go will only result in splitting the wood. Always remember to work to the centre.

4 Although the method for cutting all the joints is the same, check the drawings to see which face the joints are on.

5 When all the joints for one side wall have been cut, test assemble the wall and clean

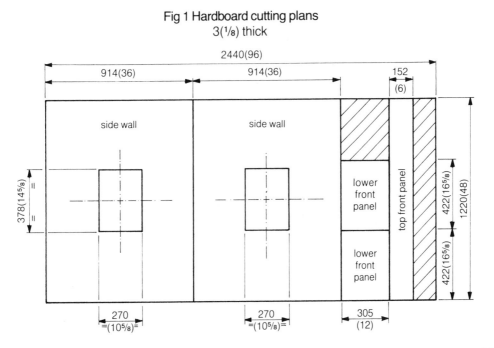

Fig 1 Hardboard cutting plans
3(⅛) thick

## Fig 2 Hardboard cutting plans

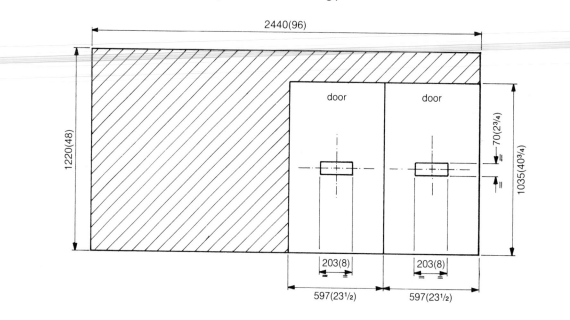

## Fig 3 Assembled side wall frame

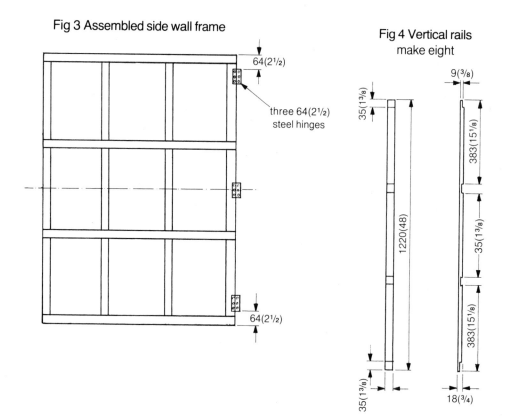

## Fig 4 Vertical rails
make eight

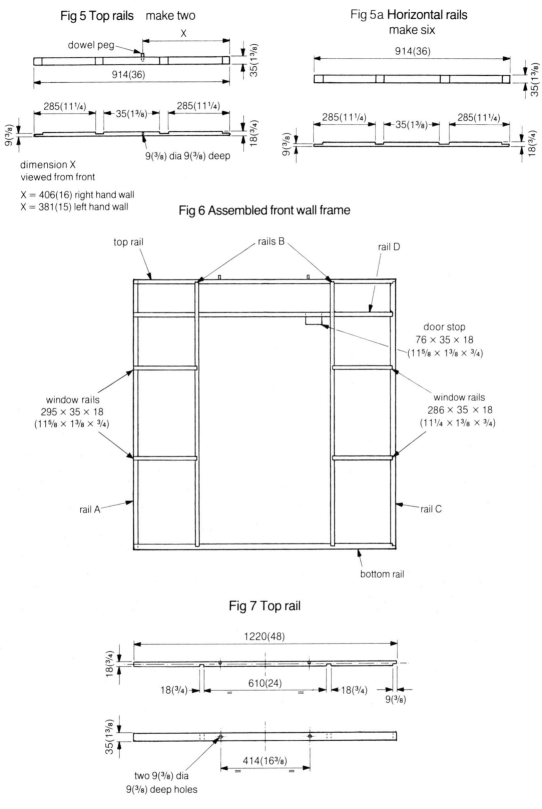

## Fig 5 Top rails   make two

X

dowel peg

35(1³⁄₈)

914(36)

285(11¼)   35(1³⁄₈)   285(11¼)

9(³⁄₈)

18(³⁄₄)

9(³⁄₈) dia 9(³⁄₈) deep

dimension X
viewed from front

X = 406(16) right hand wall
X = 381(15) left hand wall

## Fig 5a Horizontal rails
make six

914(36)

35(1³⁄₈)

285(11¼)   35(1³⁄₈)   285(11¼)

9(³⁄₈)

18(³⁄₄)

## Fig 6 Assembled front wall frame

top rail

rails B

rail D

door stop
76 × 35 × 18
(11⁵⁄₈ × 1³⁄₈ × ³⁄₄)

window rails
295 × 35 × 18
(11⁵⁄₈ × 1³⁄₈ × ³⁄₄)

window rails
286 × 35 × 18
(11¼ × 1³⁄₈ × ³⁄₄)

rail A

rail C

bottom rail

## Fig 7 Top rail

1220(48)

18(³⁄₄)

18(³⁄₄)   610(24)   18(³⁄₄)

9(³⁄₈)

35(1³⁄₈)

414(16³⁄₈)

two 9(³⁄₈) dia
9(³⁄₈) deep holes

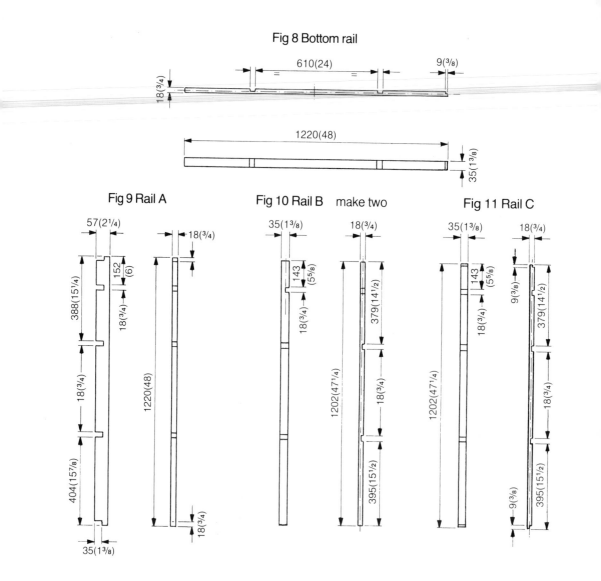

Fig 8 Bottom rail

Fig 9 Rail A

Fig 10 Rail B make two

Fig 11 Rail C

out any joints where necessary. When you are satisfied your joints are a good tight fit, dismantle and re-assemble using glue.

6 Place the assembled wall frame on to the smooth face of the hardboard wall and using a pencil, mark around the frame. This will give you a guide when pinning the two parts together. Now cover the frame with glue, place the hardboard wall on to the frame and using 20mm (¾in) panel pins, pin the two together. Use a nail punch to tap the heads of the panel pins below the surface of the hardboard.

7 Make the remaining side and front walls using the methods previously described. The door (Fig 13) is also made using these

methods but it has hardboard on both sides, and wood pinned and glued around the mail box opening.

8 When all the walls are complete, lay them side by side and screw the hinges in position.

9 Now stand the house upright and position the side walls at 90° to the front wall. Mark and drill the dowel holes in the top rail of the front wall and glue dowels in position. Place the braces (Fig 18) over the dowels and position them at 45° to the front wall. Mark and drill the dowel holes on the side walls, and glue dowels in position.

Fitting the braces in this way will give

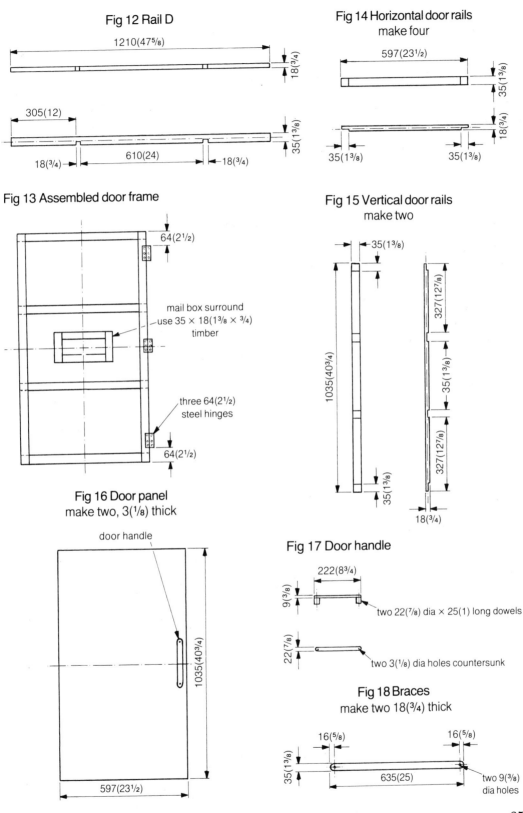

**Fig 12 Rail D**

1210(47⁵⁄₈)
18(³⁄₄)
305(12)
35(1³⁄₈)
18(³⁄₄)
610(24)
18(³⁄₄)

**Fig 13 Assembled door frame**

64(2¹⁄₂)

mail box surround
use 35 × 18(1³⁄₈ × ³⁄₄)
timber

three 64(2¹⁄₂)
steel hinges

64(2¹⁄₂)

**Fig 16 Door panel**
make two, 3(¹⁄₈) thick

door handle

1035(40³⁄₄)

597(23¹⁄₂)

**Fig 14 Horizontal door rails**
make four

597(23¹⁄₂)
35(1³⁄₈)
18(³⁄₄)
35(1³⁄₈)
35(1³⁄₈)

**Fig 15 Vertical door rails**
make two

35(1³⁄₈)
327(12⁷⁄₈)
1035(40³⁄₄)
35(1³⁄₈)
327(12⁷⁄₈)
35(1³⁄₈)
18(³⁄₄)

**Fig 17 Door handle**

222(8³⁄₄)
9(³⁄₈)
two 22(⁷⁄₈) dia × 25(1) long dowels

22(⁷⁄₈)
two 3(¹⁄₈) dia holes countersunk

**Fig 18 Braces**
make two 18(³⁄₄) thick

16(⁵⁄₈)
16(⁵⁄₈)
35(1³⁄₈)
635(25)
two 9(³⁄₈)
dia holes

accurate positioning.

10 To fit the door to the front wall, screw the hinges to the door and support it in position using pieces of scrap wood under the bottom of it to get the correct height.

11 Make and fit door handle, drilling a 3mm (1/8in) countersunk hole through each end in the centre of the 22mm (7/8in) dia dowel. A pilot hole will have to be drilled through the hardboard to give the screws a start.

12 Make and fit a door stop.

13 Last but not least, a 9mm (3/8in) dia hole has to be drilled through the window frame and into the opening edge of the door. A 9mm (3/8in) dia dowel is placed into the door through the window frame to stop the door swinging open when being carried. The position of this hole is in the middle of the lower window.

## Cutting list

Front wall top & bottom

| | | | |
|---|---|---|---|
| rails (Figs 7 and 8) | 1 each | 1220×35×18mm (48×1⅜×¾in) | Wood |
| rail A (Fig 9) | 1 off | 1220×57×25mm (48×2¼×1in) | Wood |
| rail B and C (Figs 10 and 11) | 3 off | 1200×35×18mm (47¼×1⅜×¾in) | Wood |
| rail D (Fig 12) | 1 off | 1210×35×18mm (47⅝×1⅜×¾in) | Wood |
| window rails | 2 off | 286×35×18mm (11¼×1⅜×¾in) | Wood |
| | 2 off | 295×35×18mm (11⅝×1⅜×¾in) | Wood |
| door stop | 1 off | 76×35×18mm (3×1⅜×¾in) | Wood |
| lower panels (Fig 1) | 2 off | 305×422×3mm (12×16⅝×⅛in) | Hardboard |
| top panel (Fig 1) | 1 off | 1220×152×3mm (48×6×⅛in) | Hardboard |
| dowel pegs | 2 off | 32mm(1¼in)long×9mm(3/8in)dia dowel | |

Side walls, vertical

| | | | |
|---|---|---|---|
| rails (Fig 4) | 8 off | 1220×35×18mm (48×1⅜×¾in) | Wood |
| horizontal rails (Fig 5a) | 8 off | 914×35×18mm (36×1⅜×¾in) | Wood |
| wall panels (Fig 1) | 2 off | 1220×914×3mm (48×36×⅛in) | Hardboard |
| dowel pegs | 2 off | 32mm(1¼in)long×9mm(3/8in)dia dowel | |

Door, horizontal rails

| | | | |
|---|---|---|---|
| (Fig 14) | 4 off | 597×35×18mm (23½×1⅜×¾in) | Wood |
| vertical rails (Fig 15) | 2 off | 1035×35×18mm (40¾×1⅜×¾in) | Wood |
| mail box surround (Fig 13) | 2 off | 203×35×18mm (8×1⅜×¾in) | Wood |
| | 2 off | 139×35×18mm (5½×1⅜×¾in) | Wood |
| door handle (Fig 17) | 1 off | 222×22×9mm (8¾×⅞×3/8in) | Wood |
| | 2 off | 25mm(1in)long×22mm(7/8in)dia dowel | |
| door panels (Fig 16) | 2 off | 597×1035×3mm (23½×40¾×⅛in) | Hardboard |
| Braces (Fig 18) | 2 off | 635×35×18mm (25×1⅜×¾in) | Wood |

*Ancillaries*

| | |
|---|---|
| 9 off | 64mm (2½in) long hinges |
| | 20mm (¾in) gauge panel pins |

*Supersonic Airliner (see page 24), Alpha Space Fighter (see page 27) and International Airport (see page 110)*

# GARAGE
*(shown in colour opposite)*

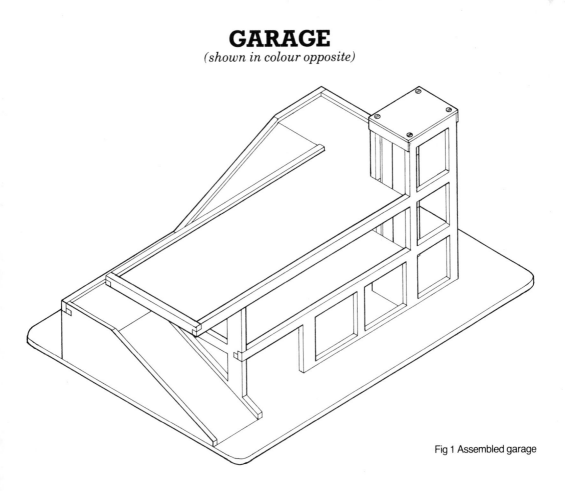

Fig 1 Assembled garage

This garage is a good addition to any young boy's toy car collection and it will help him to develop his sense of play.

He can winch his cars up to their parking place or he can simply drive them all the way to the top.

When he has parked all his vehicles, an emergency occurs and the fire engines, police vehicles and ambulances come out at top speed from their special emergency bays with their own opening doors, at the rear of the garage, just like the real thing!

1 Cut out baseboard (Fig 2) and round off the corners.
2 As will be seen from the baseboard plan, the garage is made up from three struc-

*Garage (above)*

tures, the ground floor ramp, the lift assembly and front wall, and the emergency vehicle bays. It is best to build all structures before marking and drilling their positions on the baseboard.
3 Start by cutting out and making up the ground floor ramp structure (Fig 3). The hardboard roadway will have to be chamfered at both ends to lie snug against the baseboard and lower deck.
4 It is essential when assembling each unit, to make sure that they are true, otherwise problems will occur when fitting them all together.
5 Before assembling the front wall (Fig 4) and lift wall (Fig 5) as a whole, check that the lift car (Fig 6) runs free in its guides.
6 The guides at the rear of the lift car are made from plastic door track which has been cut to leave an 'L' shape. These guides are attached with a contact adhesive.

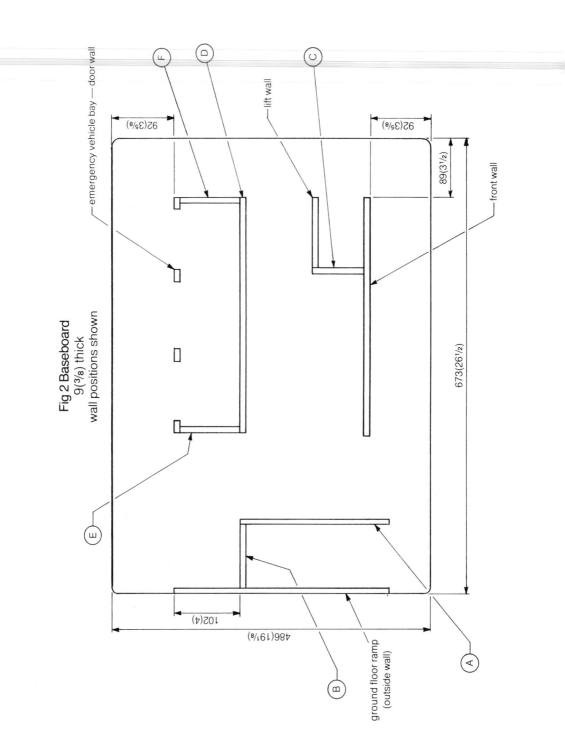

Fig 2 Baseboard
9(3/8) thick
wall positions shown

emergency vehicle bay — door wall

lift wall

front wall

ground floor ramp
(outside wall)

92(3⁵/₈)

92(3⁵/₈)

89(3¹/₂)

673(26¹/₂)

102(4)

486(19¹/₈)

A

B

C

D

E

F

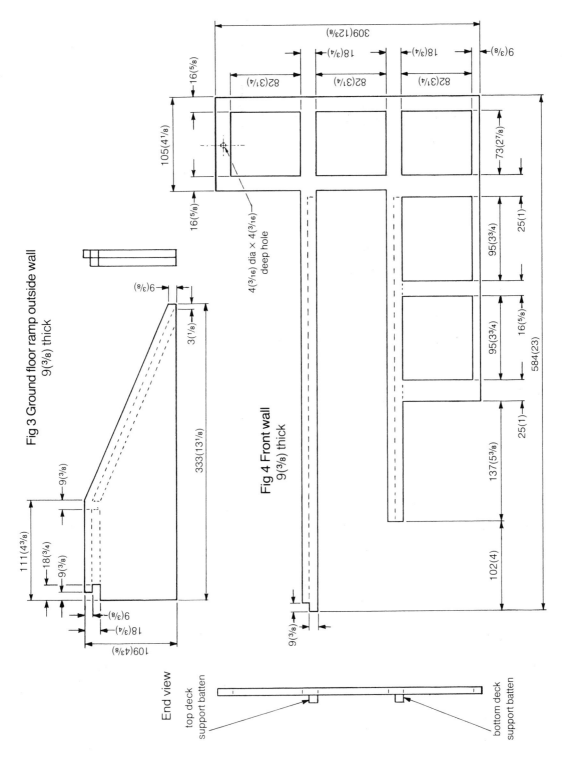

Fig 3 Ground floor ramp outside wall
9(³⁄₈) thick

Fig 4 Front wall
9(³⁄₈) thick

End view

top deck support batten

bottom deck support batten

4(³⁄₁₆) dia × 4(³⁄₁₆) deep hole

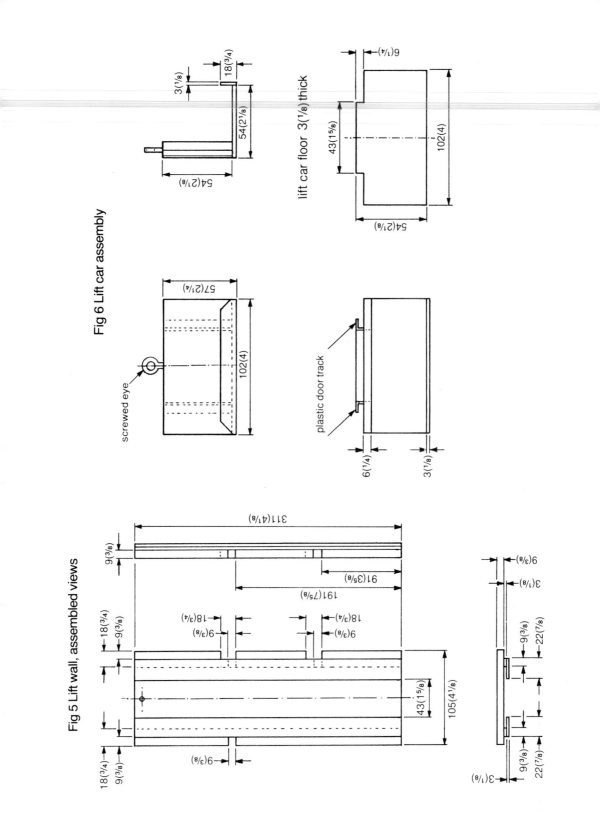

Fig 6 Lift car assembly

lift car floor 3(1/8) thick

screwed eye

plastic door track

Fig 5 Lift wall, assembled views

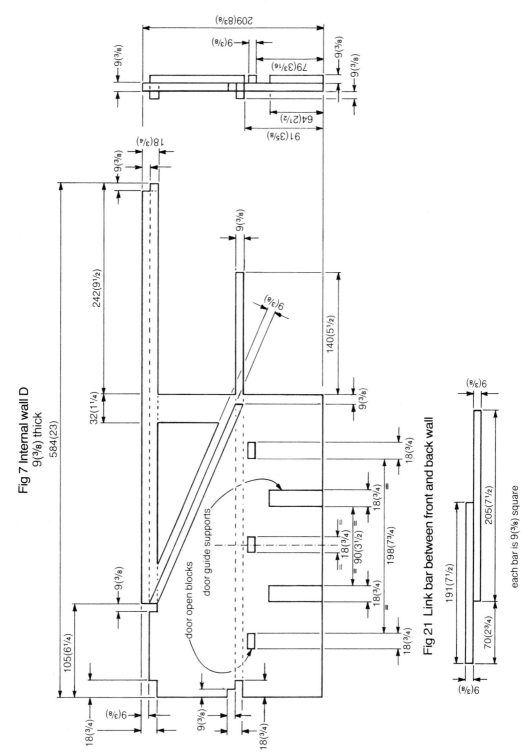

Fig 7 Internal wall D
9(³/₈) thick

584(23)

242(9½)

32(1¼)

105(6¼)

18(³/₄)

9(³/₈)

9(³/₈)

9(³/₈)

18(³/₄)

9(³/₈)

9(³/₈)

18(³/₄)

door open blocks

door guide supports

140(5½)

9(³/₈)

9(³/₈)

18(³/₄)

18(³/₄)

198(7¾)

90(3½)

18(³/₄)

18(³/₄)

18(³/₄)

209(8³/₈)

9(³/₈)

79(3³/₁₆)

9(³/₈)

9(³/₈)

64(2½)

91(3⁵/₈)

Fig 21 Link bar between front and back wall

9(³/₈)

205(7½)

191(7½)

70(2¾)

9(³/₈)

each bar is 9(³/₈) square

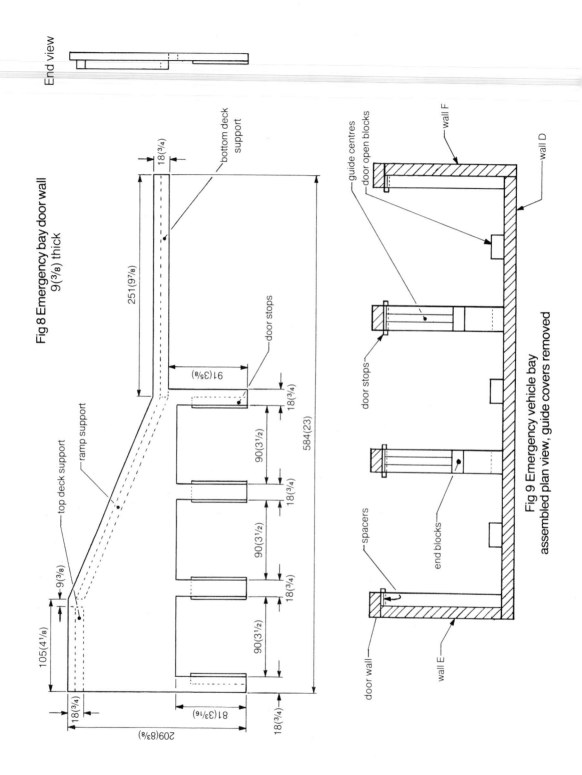

End view

## Fig 8 Emergency bay door wall
9(3/8) thick

top deck support

ramp support

bottom deck support

door stops

18(3/4)

251(9⁷/₈)

91(3⁵/₈)

9(3/8)

105(4¹/₈)

18(3/4)

209(8³/₈)

81(3³/₁₆)

90(3¹/₂)

18(3/4)

90(3¹/₂)

18(3/4)

90(3¹/₂)

18(3/4)

584(23)

## Fig 9 Emergency vehicle bay
assembled plan view, guide covers removed

guide centres

door open blocks

door stops

spacers

end blocks

door wall

wall E

wall F

wall D

Fig 10 Assembled end view
guide covers shown

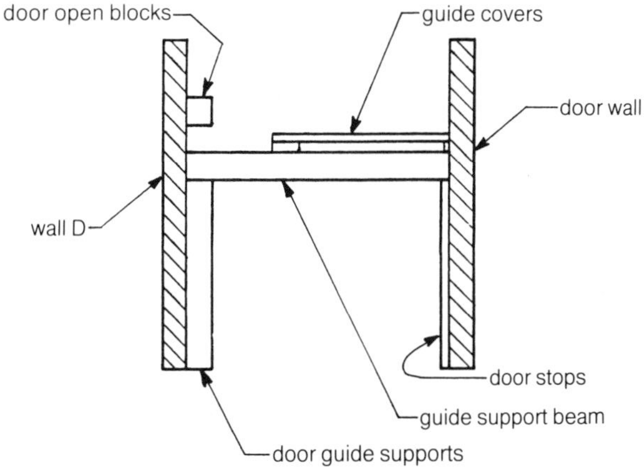
door open blocks
guide covers
door wall
wall D
door stops
guide support beam
door guide supports

Fig 11 Emergency vehicle bay doors
3(1/8) thick

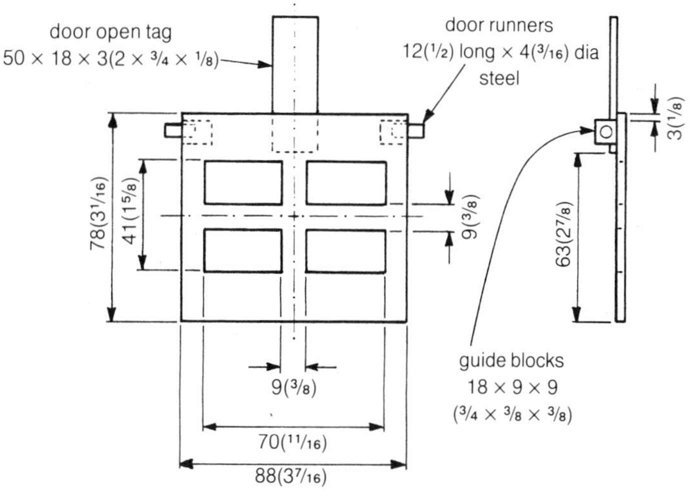
door open tag
50 × 18 × 3(2 × 3/4 × 1/8)
door runners
12(1/2) long × 4(3/16) dia
steel
3(1/8)
78(3 1/16)
41(1 5/8)
9(3/8)
63(2 7/8)
guide blocks
18 × 9 × 9
(3/4 × 3/8 × 3/8)
9(3/8)
70(11/16)
88(3 7/16)

Fig 12 Guide gap filler

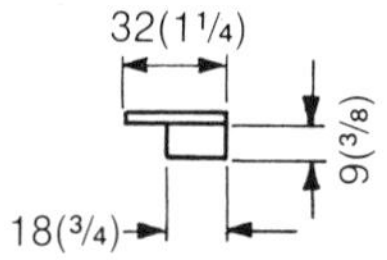
32(1 1/4)
9(3/8)
18(3/4)

7 Cut out and assemble internal wall D (Fig 7) and emergency bay door-wall (Fig 8) to form the second ramp and the emergency vehicle bays (Figs 9 and 10).

8 The opening doors (Fig 11) are pivoted on a 4mm (3/16in) dia steel rod and these need to run freely through the guides. The door open tags on the top of the doors need to sit underneath the door open blocks which are fitted to wall D, when the door is in the open position.

9 Do not fit the guide covers or the small guide fillers (Fig 12), until painting has been completed and the doors are ready for installation.

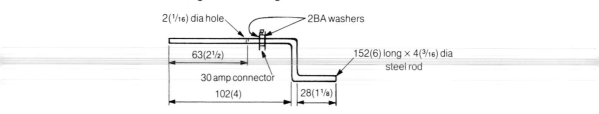

## Fig 13 Lift winding handle

2($^1$/₁₆) dia hole
2BA washers
63(2½)
152(6) long × 4(³/₁₆) dia
steel rod
30 amp connector
102(4)
28(1⅛)

Internal wall B 93 × 100 × 9(3⅞ × 4 × ⅜)
Internal wall C 79 × 100 × 9(3⅛ × 4 × ⅜)

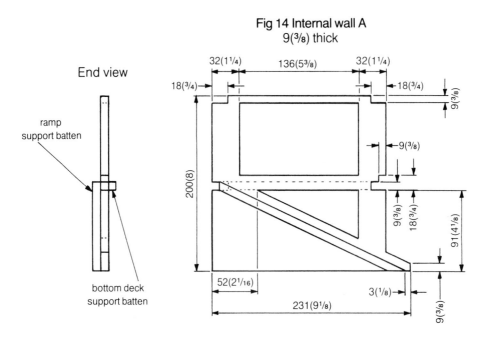

### Fig 14 Internal wall A
9(⅜) thick

End view

ramp
support batten

bottom deck
support batten

32(1¼)  136(5⅜)  32(1¼)

18(¾)  18(¾)

9(⅜)

200(8)

9(⅜)  18(¾)  91(4⅛)

9(⅜)

52(2¹/₁₆)  3(⅛)

231(9⅛)

9(⅜)

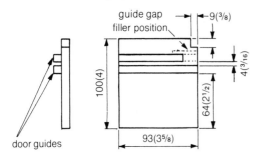

### Fig 15 Internal wall E
9(⅜) thick

guide gap
filler position
9(⅜)

4(³/₁₆)

100(4)

64(2½)

door guides

93(3⅝)

10 Do not glue into position (with the exception of the lower ramp roadway) any roadways or decks until painting has been completed. This will make the job a lot easier. Make sure to keep all deck support beams free of paint.

11 The lift handle (Fig 13) is made from a 4mm (³/₁₆in) dia steel rod. It passes through the rear lift wall, and locates into a recess on the front wall. It has to be a tight fit in the rear wall otherwise the lift car will not stay in an off-ground position. To secure the handle in position a 30amp electrical connector is used. First strip the plastic insulation from it and then cut it in half. The screw thread will also have to be

## Fig 16 External wall F
### 9(³/₈) thick

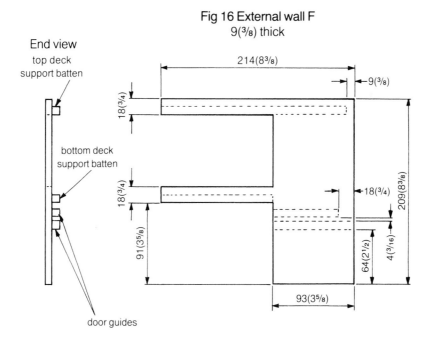

End view

top deck
support batten

bottom deck
support batten

door guides

## Fig 17 Pump island

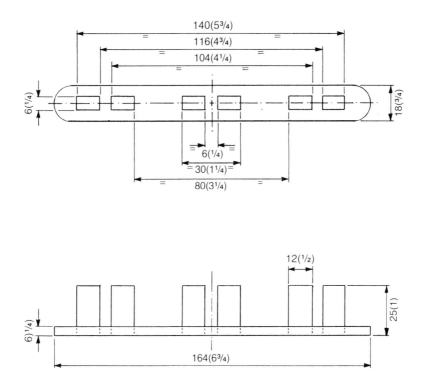

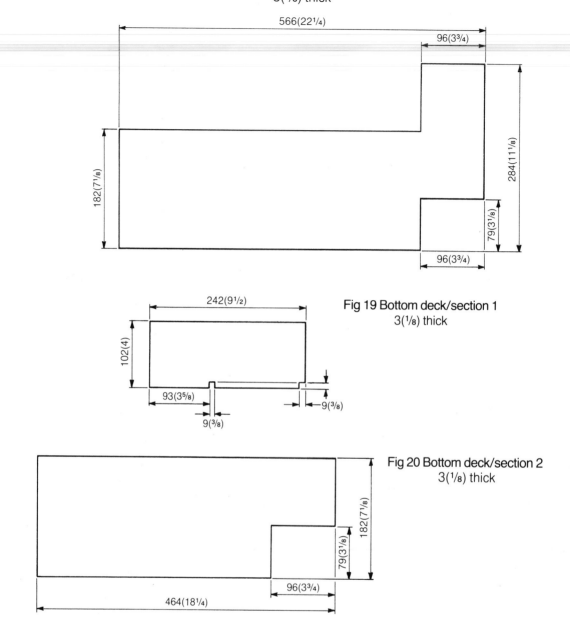

Fig 18 Top deck
3($\frac{1}{8}$) thick

566(22$\frac{1}{4}$)

96(3$\frac{3}{4}$)

284(11$\frac{1}{8}$)

182(7$\frac{1}{8}$)

79(3$\frac{1}{8}$)

96(3$\frac{3}{4}$)

Fig 19 Bottom deck/section 1
3($\frac{1}{8}$) thick

242(9$\frac{1}{2}$)

102(4)

93(3$\frac{5}{8}$)

9($\frac{3}{8}$)

9($\frac{3}{8}$)

Fig 20 Bottom deck/section 2
3($\frac{1}{8}$) thick

182(7$\frac{1}{8}$)

79(3$\frac{1}{8}$)

96(3$\frac{3}{4}$)

464(18$\frac{1}{4}$)

98

cut, leaving enough to clear the roof when in position. Whipping twine is used for the lift cable and this is passed through the 2mm (1/16in) dia hole and is knotted. The 2 BA washers stop the twine from riding over the connector.

12 The lift roof is secured by screws only, no glue should be used here. This is so that in the event of a cable breakage it can be repaired easily.

13 Make up the pump island as shown in Fig 17 and position on base where desired.

14 Place all assembled structures on the baseboard in their correct positions, mark around them and drill fixing holes 3mm (1/8in) diameter and countersink them. Place ramps and decks in position when marking out.

## Cutting list

| | | | |
|---|---|---|---|
| Baseboard (Fig 2) | 1 off | 673×486×9mm (26½×19⅛×⅜in) | Plywood |
| Front wall (Fig 4) | 1 off | 584×309×9mm (23×12⅜×⅜in) | Plywood |
| Bottom deck support batten | 1 off | 368×9×9mm (14½×⅜×⅜in) | Wood |
| Top deck support batten | 1 off | 461×9×9mm (18⅛×⅜×⅜in) | Wood |
| Internal wall A (Fig 14) | 1 off | 231×200×9mm (9⅛×8×⅜in) | Plywood |
| Ramp support | 1 off | 243×9×9mm (9⁹/16×⅜×⅜in) | Wood |
| Bottom deck support | 1 off | 164×9×9mm (6⅜×⅜×⅜in) | Wood |
| Ground floor ramp (outside wall) (Fig 3) | 1 off | 333×109×9mm (13⅛×4⅜×⅜in) | Plywood |
| Ramp support | 1 off | 243×9×9mm (9⁹/16×⅜×⅜in) | Wood |
| Bottom deck support | 1 off | 84×9×9mm (3¼×⅜×⅜in) | Plywood |
| Internal wall B | 1 off | 93×100×9mm (3⅝×4×⅜in) | Plywood |
| Internal wall C | 1 off | 79×100×9mm (3⅛×4×⅜in) | Plywood |
| Internal wall E (Fig 15) | 1 off | 93×100×9mm (3⅝×4×⅜in) | Plywood |
| Battens | 1 off | 93×9×9mm (3⅝×⅜×⅜in) | Wood |
| Battens | 1 off | 77×9×9mm (3×⅜×⅜in) | Wood |
| External wall F (Fig 16) | 1 off | 214×209×9mm (8⅜×8⅜×⅜in) | Plywood |
| Battens | 1 off | 205×9×9mm (8×⅜×⅜in) | Wood |
| Battens | 1 off | 121×9×9mm (4¾×⅜×⅜in) | Wood |
| Battens | 1 off | 93×9×9mm (3⅝×⅜×⅜in) | Wood |
| Battens | 1 off | 75×9×9mm (2⅞×⅜×⅜in) | Wood |
| Internal wall D (Fig 7) | 1 off | 584×209×9mm (23×8⅜×⅜in) | Plywood |
| Bottom deck support | 1 off | 464×9×9mm (18¼×⅜×⅜in) | Wood |
| Top deck support | 1 off | 470×9×9mm (18½×⅜×⅜in) | Wood |
| Door guide supports | 2 off | 64×18×9mm (2½×¾×⅜in) | Plywood |
| Door open blocks | 3 off | 18×9×9mm (¾×⅜×⅜in) | Wood |
| Ramp support | 1 off | 251×9×9mm (9⅞×⅜×⅜in) | Wood |
| Emergency bay door wall (Fig 8) | 1 off | 584×209×9mm (23×8⅜×⅜in) | Plywood |
| Top deck support | 1 off | 77×9×9mm (3×⅜×⅜in) | Wood |
| Ramp support | 1 off | 251×9×9mm (9⅞×⅜×⅜in) | Wood |
| Bottom deck support | 1 off | 251×9×9mm (9⅞×⅜×⅜in) | Wood |
| Spacers (Fig 9) | 2 off | 18×9×2mm (¾×⅜×1/16in) | Plywood |
| Spacer | 2 off | 9×9×2mm (⅜×⅜×1/16in) | Plywood |
| Door stops middle pillars | 2 off | 25×64×3mm (1×2½×⅛in) | Plywood |
| Door stops end pillars | 2 off | 12×64×3mm (½×2½×⅛in) | Plywood |
| Lift wall (Fig 5) | 1 off | 105×311×9mm (4⅛×12⅛×⅜in) | Plywood |
| Lift guides | 2 off | 9×311×3mm (⅜×12⅛×⅛in) | Plywood |
| | 2 off | 22×311×3mm (⅞×12⅛×⅛in) | Plywood |

| | | | |
|---|---|---|---|
| Roof | 1 off | 111×88×3mm (4³⁄₈×3¹⁄₂×¹⁄₈in) | Hardboard |
| | 2 off | 88×18×3mm (4³⁄₈×³⁄₄×¹⁄₈in) | Hardboard |
| Lift car floor (Fig 6) | 1 off | 102×54×3mm (4×2¹⁄₈×¹⁄₈in) | Plywood |
| Back wall | 1 off | 102×54×6mm (4×2¹⁄₈×¹⁄₄in) | Plywood |
| Spacer block | 1 off | 43×54×6mm (1⁵⁄₈×2¹⁄₈×¹⁄₄in) | Plywood |
| Front wall | 1 off | 102×18×3mm (4×³⁄₄×¹⁄₈in) | Plywood |
| Pump island base (Fig 17) | 1 off | 164×18×6mm (6³⁄₄×³⁄₄×¹⁄₄in) | Plywood |
| Pumps | 6 off | 12×25×6mm (¹⁄₂×1×¹⁄₄in) | Plywood |
| Link bar between front wall and back wall (Fig 21) | 1 off | 191×9×9mm (7¹⁄₂×³⁄₈×³⁄₈in) | Wood |
| | 1 off | 205×9×9mm (8×³⁄₈×³⁄₈in) | Wood |
| Emergency vehicle bay doors (Fig 11) | 3 off | 88×78×3mm (3⁷⁄₁₆×3¹⁄₁₆×¹⁄₈in) | Plywood |
| Door open tags | 3 off | 18×50×3mm (³⁄₄×2×¹⁄₈in) | Plywood |
| Guide blocks | 6 off | 18×9×9mm (³⁄₄×³⁄₈×³⁄₈in) | Wood |
| Guide centres | 2 off | 57×6×4mm (2¹⁄₄×¹⁄₄×³⁄₁₆in) | Plywood |
| End blocks | 2 off | 18×9×4mm (³⁄₄×³⁄₈×³⁄₁₆in) | Plywood |
| Guide covers | 2 off | 66×18×3mm (2⁵⁄₈×³⁄₄×¹⁄₈in) | Plywood |
| Guide support beam | 2 off | 93×18×9mm (3⁵⁄₈×³⁄₄×³⁄₈in) | Wood |
| Guide gap fillers (Fig 12) | 2 off | 32×9×3mm (1¹⁄₄×³⁄₈×¹⁄₈in) | Plywood |
| | 2 off | 18×9×9mm (³⁄₄×³⁄₈×³⁄₈in) | Plywood |
| Top deck (Fig 18) | 1 off | 566×284×3mm (22¹⁄₄×11¹⁄₈×¹⁄₈in) | Hardboard |
| Bottom deck/section 1 (Fig 19) | 1 off | 242×102×3mm (9¹⁄₂×4×¹⁄₈in) | Hardboard |
| Bottom deck/section 2 (Fig 20) | 1 off | 464×182×3mm (18¹⁄₄×7¹⁄₈×¹⁄₈in) | Hardboard |
| Ground floor ramp | 1 off | 245×93×3mm (9⁵⁄₈×3⁵⁄₈×¹⁄₈in) | Hardboard |
| Top floor ramp | 1 off | 251×93×3mm (9⁷⁄₈×3⁵⁄₈×¹⁄₈in) | Hardboard |

*Ancilliaries*

| | | |
|---|---|---|
| Plastic door track | | 108mm (4¹⁄₄in) long |
| Chromed screwed eye | 1 off | |
| 2BA washers | 2 off | |
| 30 Amp electrical connector | 1 off | |
| Lift winding handle (Fig 13) | 1 off | 152mm(6in)long×4mm(³⁄₁₆in)dia metal rod |
| Emergency vehicle bay door runners | 6 off | 12mm(¹⁄₂in)long×4mm(³⁄₁₆in)dia metal rod |
| Lift cable | | 356mm (14in) long whipping twine |

# PONY STABLE

*(shown in colour on page 52)*

A toy which is very popular with young girls is the 'My Little-Pony' figure. When my daughter asked for a stable to go with her little pony, naturally a stable of suitable size had to be built. To compliment the stable, fences, jumps, a bed and vanity table have been made.

The roof is completely removable to allow play inside, and all the accessories can be kept here when not in use.

1 Mark and cut out the base (Fig 1), front and back walls (Figs 2 and 3). For method of how to cut window and door openings refer to page 9.

2 Now cut the two side walls (Fig 4). The roof shape for these walls is made by cutting each top edge at 45°.

3 Test assemble the walls on to the base. Cut the four corner blocks to length. Glue the walls to the base and allow to harden.

4 Cut the four main roof sections (*see* Figs 5–8) to size and glue the roof corner blocks to the two outside roof sections.

5 Place one outside roof section with its inside partner in position and glue and

Fig 1 Base
6($\frac{1}{4}$) thick

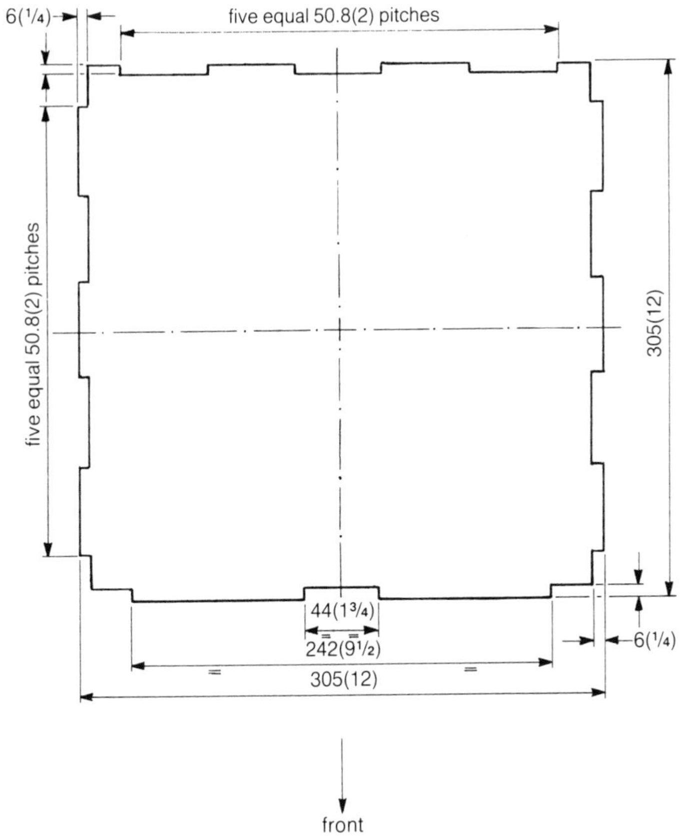

6($\frac{1}{4}$)

five equal 50.8(2) pitches

five equal 50.8(2) pitches

305(12)

44(1$\frac{3}{4}$)

242(9$\frac{1}{2}$)

305(12)

6($\frac{1}{4}$)

front

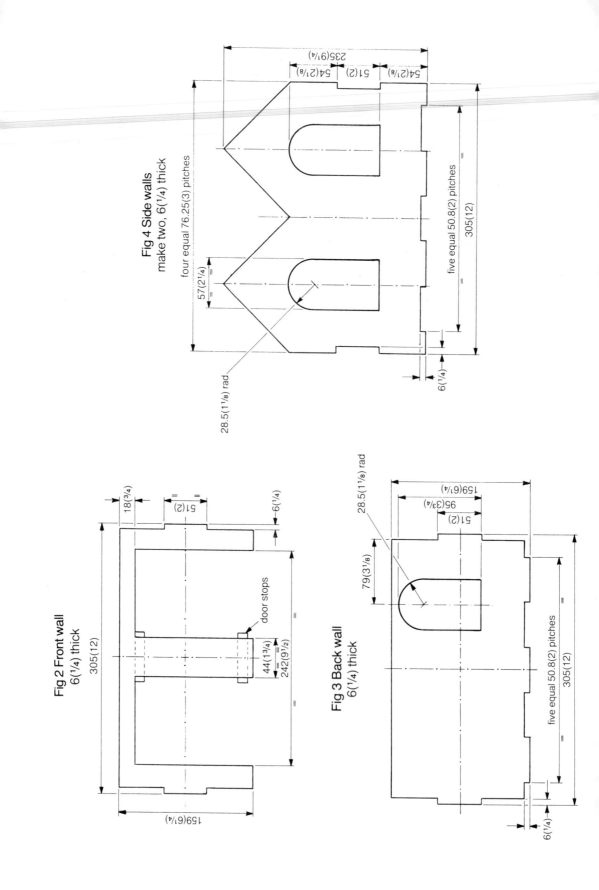

**Fig 4 Side walls**
make two, 6(¹/₄) thick

four equal 76.25(3) pitches

235(9¹/₄)

54(2¹/₈)  51(2)  54(2¹/₈)

305(12)

five equal 50.8(2) pitches

57(2¹/₄)

28.5(1¹/₈) rad

6(¹/₄)

**Fig 2 Front wall**
6(¹/₄) thick

305(12)

159(6¹/₄)

18(³/₄)

51(2)

6(¹/₄)

door stops

44(1³/₄)

242(9¹/₂)

**Fig 3 Back wall**
6(¹/₄) thick

28.5(1¹/₈) rad

159(6¹/₄)

95(3³/₄)

51(2)

79(3¹/₈)

305(12)

five equal 50.8(2) pitches

6(¹/₄)

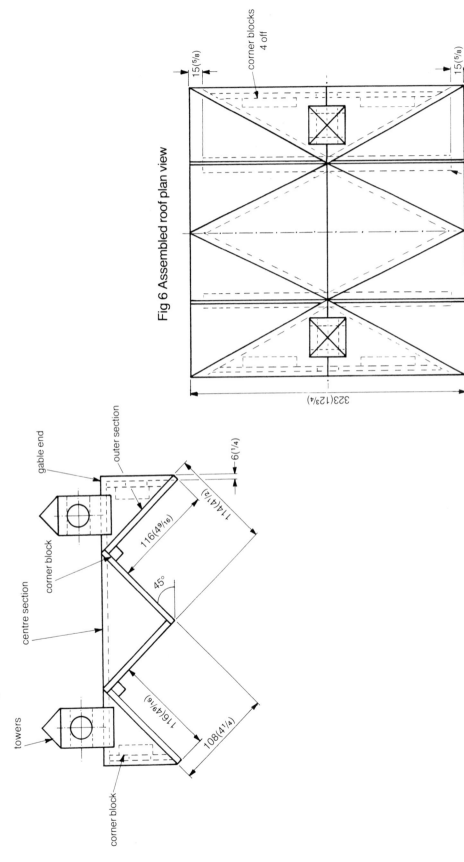

Fig 5 Assembled roof side view

Fig 6 Assembled roof plan view

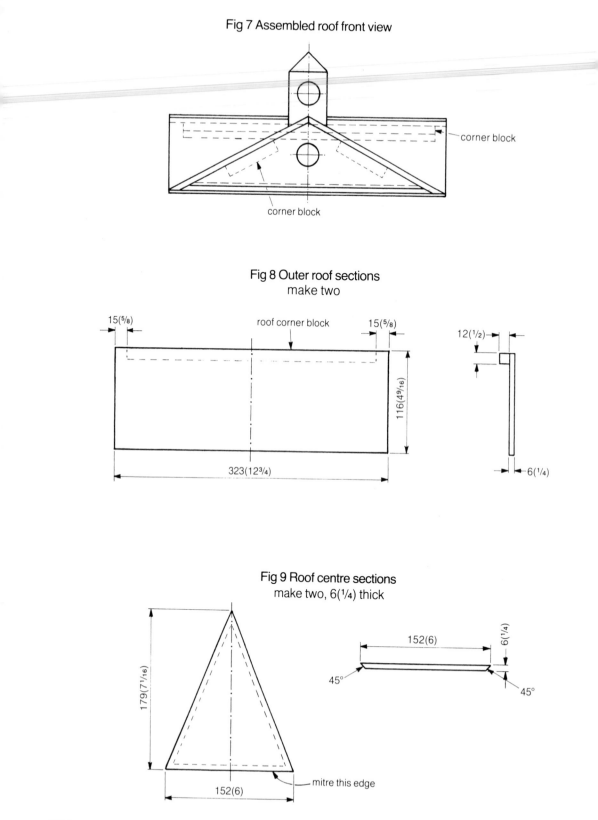

Fig 7 Assembled roof front view

corner block

corner block

Fig 8 Outer roof sections
make two

15(⁵⁄₈)

roof corner block

15(⁵⁄₈)

12(¹⁄₂)

116(4⁹⁄₁₆)

323(12³⁄₄)

6(¹⁄₄)

Fig 9 Roof centre sections
make two, 6(¹⁄₄) thick

179(7¹⁄₁₆)

152(6)

6(¹⁄₄)

45°

45°

152(6)

mitre this edge

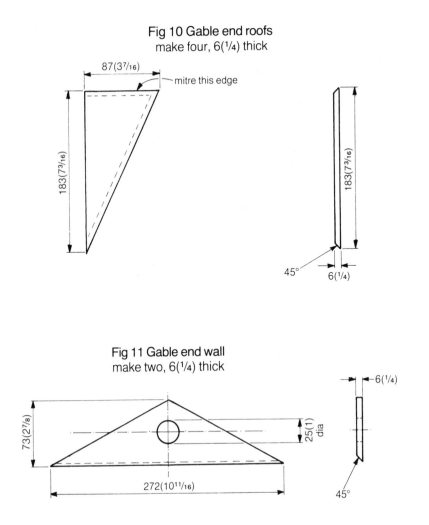

Fig 10 Gable end roofs
make four, 6(¼) thick

87(3⁷/₁₆)

mitre this edge

183(7³/₁₆)

183(7³/₁₆)

45°

6(¼)

Fig 11 Gable end wall
make two, 6(¼) thick

6(¼)

73(2⁷/₈)

25(1)
dia

272(10¹¹/₁₆)

45°

cramp them together. Repeat this process for the remaining two roof sections. Then carefully glue the two completed sections together.

6 Mark and cut out the two roof centre sections (Fig 9). Test assemble before glueing in position because the top edges have to be mitred for a snug fit.

7 When preparing the gable ends (Fig 10), exact measuring and cutting is essential. The top edges of the roofs have to be mitred, and this is done by marking their positions on the main roof section and continually testing their position as these edges are filed to shape.

When mitre is completed, glue corner blocks in position.

8 Cut the gable end walls (Fig 11) to size. Drill the 25mm (1in) dia hole using either a flat bit or hole saw (see page 13).

9 To assemble a gable end unit, lay one roof section flat and glue the wall to it. Then glue the remaining roof section in position using a block of scrap wood to support it.

Allow glue to harden and test assemble. If the unit does not sit flat on the main roof, place a sheet of abrasive paper on a flat surface and sand the whole gable end. When a good seat has been achieved, position the main roof (using supports) so that the roof section which the gable end is to be fitted to is horizontal. Then glue in position. Repeat this process for the other gable end unit.

10 The towers (Fig 12) are made from 45×45mm (1¾×1¾in) square wood. Before cutting them to length drill the two 25mm (1in) dia holes. The end of the piece of wood that the towers are to be cut from, will make up the top of the tower. This way you will find it easier to make the angled cuts at the bottom of the tower.

11 When both towers have been completed, glue them in position.

12 Mark, cut out and fit the four front stable doors (Fig 13). Leave enough of a gap around each door to allow for paint thickness. If hinge screws should protrude through walls and/or doors, file them flush.

13 To mark out the back wall door (Fig 14), draw through the window on to plywood to be used. This method will produce an accurately shaped door.

14 When making the bed, vanity table, fence and jumps (Figs 15–19), use hardwood.

15 Smooth all edges and paint.

See colour photograph on page 52 for assembled views of fence and jumps A and B.

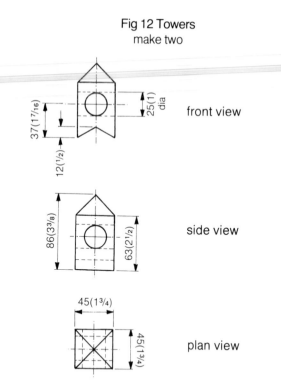

Fig 12 Towers
make two

front view

side view

plan view

## Fig 13 Front wall doors

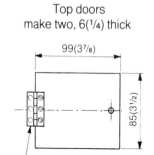

Top doors
make two, 6(¼) thick

38(1½) brass hinges
one per door

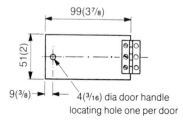

Bottom doors
make two, 6(¼) thick

4(³/₁₆) dia door handle
locating hole one per door

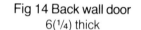

Door handles    make four 15(⅞) long × 4(⅞) dia dowel

## Fig 14 Back wall door
6(¼) thick

28.5(1⅛) rad

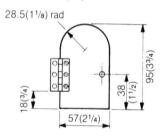

## Fig 15 Bed

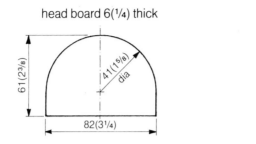

head board 6(¼) thick

61(2³/8)

41(1⁵/8) dia

82(3¼)

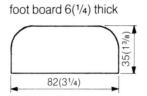

foot board 6(¼) thick

35(1³/8)

82(3¼)

Bed base 155 × 82 × 18(6⅛ × 3¼ × ¾)

## Fig 16 Vanity table
assembled views

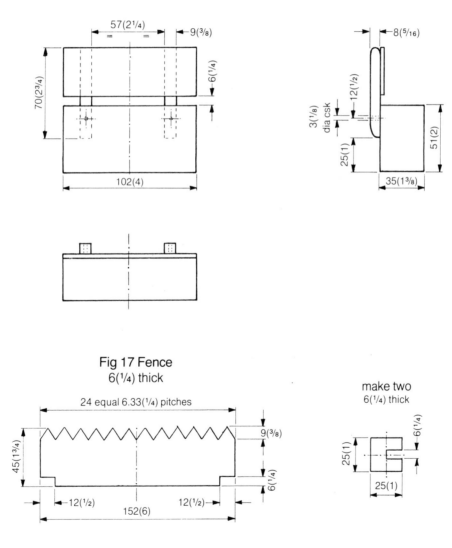

57(2¼)

9(³/8)

8(⁵/16)

70(2³/4)

6(¼)

3(⅛) dia csk

12(½)

25(1)

51(2)

102(4)

35(1³/8)

## Fig 17 Fence
6(¼) thick

make two
6(¼) thick

24 equal 6.33(¼) pitches

9(³/8)

45(1³/4)

6(¼)

12(½)

12(½)

152(6)

25(1)

6(¼)

25(1)

## Fig 18 Jump A 6(¼) thick

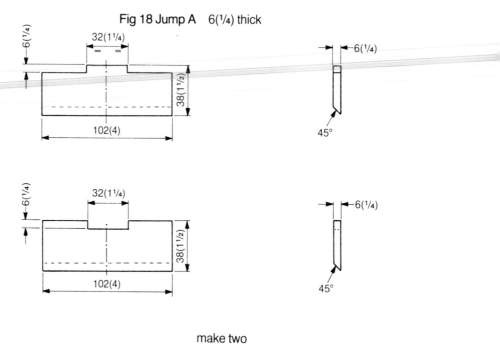

make two

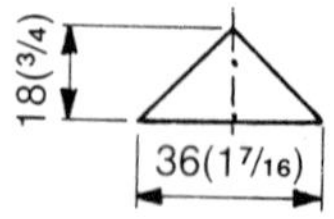

18(¾)

36(1⁷/₁₆)

## Fig 19 Jump B

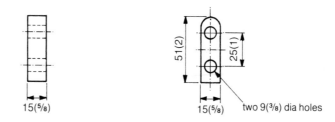

51(2)    25(1)

15(⅝)    15(⅝)    two 9(⅜) dia holes

**Jump bars**   make two 127(5) long × 9(⅜) dia dowel
**Bases**   make two 42 × 15 × 6(1⅝ × ⅝ × ¼) plywood

**Cutting list**

| | | | |
|---|---|---|---|
| Base (Fig 1) | 1 off | 305×305×6mm (12×12×¼in) | Plywood |
| Front wall (Fig 2) | 1 off | 305×159×6mm (12×6¼×¼in) | Plywood |
| Back wall (Fig 3) | 1 off | 305×159×6mm (12×6¼×¼in) | Plywood |
| Side walls (Fig 4) | 2 off | 305×235×6mm (12×9¼×¼in) | Plywood |
| Wall corner blocks | 4 off | 160×12×12mm (6¼×½×½in) | Wood |
| Roof sections (Fig 8) | 2 off | 323×116×6mm (12¾×4⁹/₁₆×¼in) | Plywood |
| | 1 off | 323×114×6mm (12¾×4½×¼in) | Plywood |
| | 1 off | 323×108×6mm (12¾×4¼×¼in) | Plywood |
| Roof corner blocks | 2 off | 293×12×12mm (11½×½×½in) | Wood |
| Roof centre sections (Fig 9) | 2 off | 179×152×6mm (7¹/₁₆×6×¼in) | Plywood |
| Gable end roofs (Fig 10) | 4 off | 183×87×6mm (7³/₁₆×3⁷/₁₆×¼in) | Plywood |
| Gable end walls (Fig 11) | 2 off | 272×73×6mm (10¹¹/₁₆×2⁷/₈×¼in) | Plywood |
| corner blocks | 4 off | 63×12×12mm (2½×½×½in) | Wood |
| Towers (Fig 12) | 2 off | 86×45×45mm (3⁵/₈×1¾×1¾in) | Wood |
| Doors, Top (Fig 13) | 2 off | 85×99×6mm (3½×3⁷/₈×¼in) | Plywood |
| Bottom (Fig 13) | 2 off | 51×99×6mm (2×3⁷/₈×¼in) | Plywood |
| Back wall door (Fig 14) | 1 off | 57×95×6mm (2¼×3¾×¼in) | Plywood |
| Handles (Fig 14) | 5 off | 15mm(⁵/₈in)long×4mm (³/₁₆in)dia dowel | |
| Door stops | 2 off | 57×12×6mm (2¼×½×¼in) | Plywood |
| | 1 off | 18×12×6mm (¾×½×¼in) | Plywood |
| Bed base (Fig 15) | 1 off | 155×82×18mm (6¹/₈×3¼×¾in) | Wood |
| headboard | 1 off | 61×82×6mm (2³/₈×3¼×¼in) | Plywood |
| footboard | 1 off | 35×82×6mm (1³/₈×3¼×¼in) | Plywood |
| Vanity table (Fig 16) | 1 off | 102×51×35mm (4×2×1³/₈in) | Hardwood |
| | 2 off | 70×8×9mm (2¾×⁵/₁₆×³/₈in) | Hardwood |
| | 1 off | 102×38×3mm (4×1½×¹/₈in) | Plywood |
| Fences (Fig 17) | 1 off | 45×152×6mm (1¾×6×¼in) | Plywood |
| | 2 off | 25×25×6mm (1×1×¼in) | Plywood |
| Jump A (Fig 18) | 2 off | 102×38×6mm (4×1½×¼in) | Plywood |
| | 2 off | 36×18×6mm (1⁷/₁₆×¹¹/₁₆×¼in) | Plywood |
| corner block | 1 off | 90×9×9mm (3½×³/₈×³/₈in) | Wood |
| Jump B (Fig 19) | 2 off | 51×15×15mm (2×⁵/₈×⁵/₈in) | Hardwood |
| | 2 off | 127mm(5in)long×9mm(³/₈in)dia dowel | |
| | 2 off | 42×15×6mm (1⁵/₈×⁵/₈×¼in) | Plywood |
| *Ancillaries* | 5 off | 38mm (1½in) brass hinges | |

# INTERNATIONAL AIRPORT

*(shown in colour on page 87)*

Large international airports can be very exciting places, especially for a child. Aeroplanes are arriving and departing all the time, flying off to far away exotic locations.

This international airport is designed to suit 1:600 scale model aeroplanes and has runway lighting to add realism for the more discerning, modern pioneer of the airways.

The batteries to power these lights are hidden away in a cargo shed building and can be quickly and easily replaced by simply removing the four screws which retain the cargo shed roof.

If you do not wish to incorporate lights into your model, simply replace the hardboard and frames shown in the directions with a plywood base, 1056×610×9mm

(41¾×24×⅜in), and start construction at section 5. To simulate runway lights use self adhesive coloured discs.

1 Cut the 35×18mm (1⅜×¾in) wood to length and cut out the joints. This will make up the frame for the hardboard base (Fig 1).

2 Drill the 3mm (⅛in) dia holes which will take the wires for the runway lights and assemble base frame.

3 Cut to size the two 1056×610×3mm (41¾×24×⅛in) hardboard panels (Figs 2 and 3). Drill twenty-two 3mm (⅛in) dia fixing holes in one of these panels (Fig 2). Pin and glue the undrilled panel (Fig 3) to the assembled frame and smooth off the edges. This panel is now the top panel.

4 Mark the positions of the runway lights

Fig 1 Base frame assembly

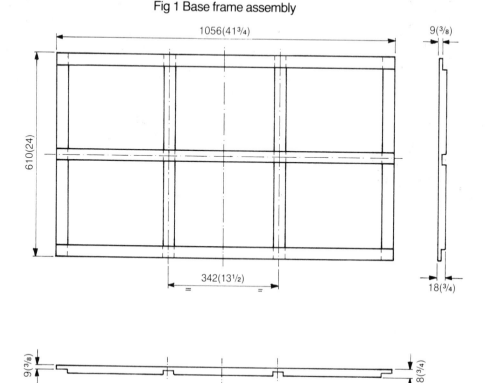

1056(41¾)

9(⅜)

610(24)

342(13½)

18(¾)

9(⅜)

18(¾)

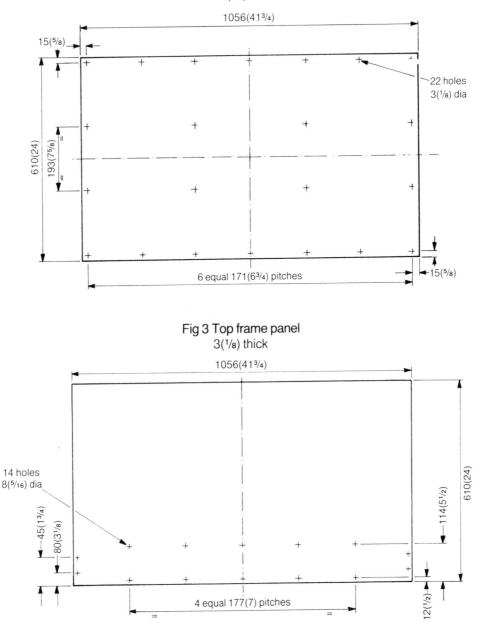

Fig 2 Bottom frame panel
3(⅛) thick

1056(41¾)

15(⅝)

610(24)

193(7⅝)

22 holes
3(⅛) dia

6 equal 171(6¾) pitches

15(⅝)

Fig 3 Top frame panel
3(⅛) thick

1056(41¾)

14 holes
8(5/16) dia

45(1¾)

80(3⅛)

610(24)

114(5½)

4 equal 177(7) pitches

12(½)

on the top panel and drill fourteen 8mm (5/16in) dia holes in these positions. Turn the base over and using a sharp knife cut a small channel from each 8mm (5/16in) dia hole (which has been drilled through the frame) towards the middle of the base. These channels must be large enough to take the wires leading from each light bulb.

5 Cut to size and make up the airport buildings (Figs 4–9). The satellite terminal can be pinned and glued together to form one unit. Position the assembled buildings on to the top panel as shown (*see*

111

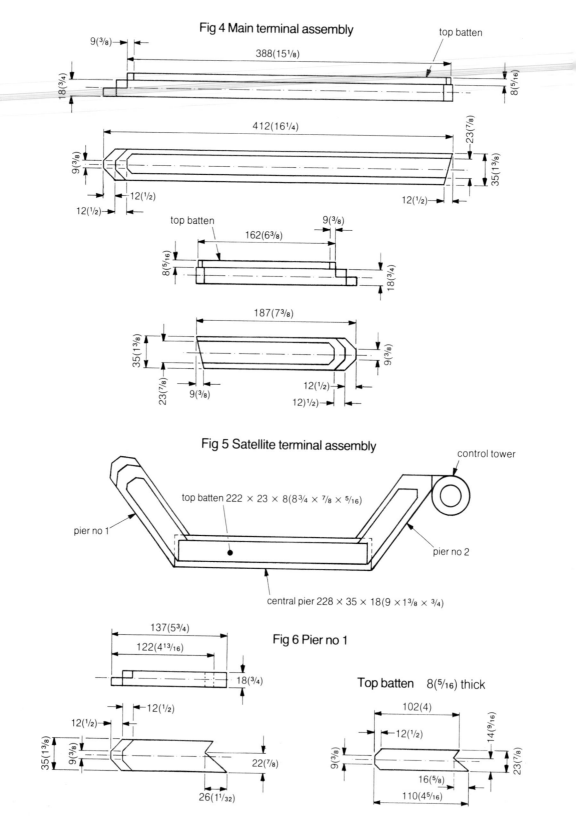

Fig 4 Main terminal assembly

top batten

9(³⁄₈)

388(15¹⁄₈)

18(³⁄₄)

8(⁵⁄₁₆)

412(16¹⁄₄)

9(³⁄₈)

23(⁷⁄₈)

35(1³⁄₈)

12(¹⁄₂)

12(¹⁄₂)

12(¹⁄₂)

top batten

9(³⁄₈)

162(6³⁄₈)

8(⁵⁄₁₆)

18(³⁄₄)

187(7³⁄₈)

35(1³⁄₈)

9(³⁄₈)

23(⁷⁄₈)

9(³⁄₈)

12(¹⁄₂)

12)¹⁄₂)

Fig 5 Satellite terminal assembly

control tower

top batten 222 × 23 × 8(8³⁄₄ × ⁷⁄₈ × ⁵⁄₁₆)

pier no 1

pier no 2

central pier 228 × 35 × 18(9 × 1³⁄₈ × ³⁄₄)

137(5³⁄₄)

Fig 6 Pier no 1

122(4¹³⁄₁₆)

18(³⁄₄)

12(¹⁄₂)

12(¹⁄₂)

Top batten    8(⁵⁄₁₆) thick

35(1³⁄₈)

9(³⁄₈)

22(⁷⁄₈)

26(1¹⁄₃₂)

102(4)

14(⁹⁄₁₆)

12(¹⁄₂)

9(³⁄₈)

23(⁷⁄₈)

16(⁵⁄₈)

110(4⁵⁄₁₆)

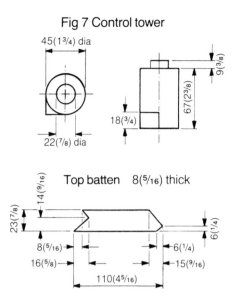

Fig 7 Control tower

45(1¾) dia
22(⅞) dia
18(¾)
67(2⅜)
9(⅜)

Top batten    8(⁵/₁₆) thick

14(⁹/₁₆)
23(⅞)
8(⁵/₁₆)
16(⅝)
6(¼)
15(⁹/₁₆)
6(¼)
110(4⁵/₁₆)

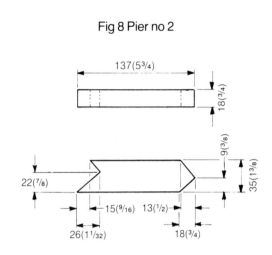

Fig 8 Pier no 2

137(5¾)
18(¾)
22(⅞)
9(⅜)
35(1⅜)
15(⁹/₁₆)  13(½)
26(1¹/₃₂)
18(¾)

Fig 10) and draw around them. Remove the buildings and using the outline as a guide, drill 5mm (³/₁₆in) fixing holes for each building, countersinking any holes that go through the frame. Reposition each building in turn and through each fixing hole mark the underside of the buildings. Now drill pilot holes into each building where they have been marked. This will enable you to position the airport buildings in their correct place after the felt and 'grass' have been glued to the base (Figs 11 and 12). When the buildings have been painted make a stencil from card (*see* Fig 11) and using a permanent marker pen, draw in the windows.

6 Three of the runway light's positions miss the frame altogether and so blocks of 50×35×18mm (2×1⅜×¾in) have to be made to house the bulbs and lenses (Fig 12). Make these blocks and pin and glue them in position.

7 Using a heavy-duty wallpaper paste cover the baseboard with the black felt. When dry, cut out the holes for the runway lights.

8 The 'grass' areas (Figs 13 and 14) are made using model railway scenic grass. Cut a pattern of the shape required on a piece of card, transfer this pattern to the scenic grass and cut out. Again using heavy-duty paste, stick the 'grass' on to the felt.

9 The runway lights are made by cutting fourteen 9mm (³/₈in) lengths from disposable ballpoint pens which have transparent stems. The tops of the lights are made from red transparent acetate sheet, glued on with cyanoacrylate glue. The four end runway lights must have their stems 'painted' with red felt pen before assembly.

When all lenses have been made, gently tap them into place until they are flush with the felt. No glue is required.

10 Feed two 1500mm (59in) lengths of 0.5mm² electrical cable through the previously drilled holes in the frame; the leftover cable is to go into the battery box (cargo shed) (Fig 9).

11 Place one 'grain of wheat' bulb into each light lense. A small wad of tissue paper is used to stop the bulb from falling out.

12 Solder each runway light to the 0.5mm² cable at the nearest convenient point. Cover each joint with PVC insulating tape.

13 Screw the buildings in place. Drill two 3mm (⅛in) dia holes through the base of the battery box (cargo shed) and feed the 0.5mm² cable through these holes and connect to the switch and battery terminals.

14 Screw the bottom hardboard panel in position.

15 The runway markings are achieved by sticking strips of masking tape to the felt and painting when in position.

## Fig 9 Battery box/cargo shed

### Side wall
make two, 9(³/₈) thick

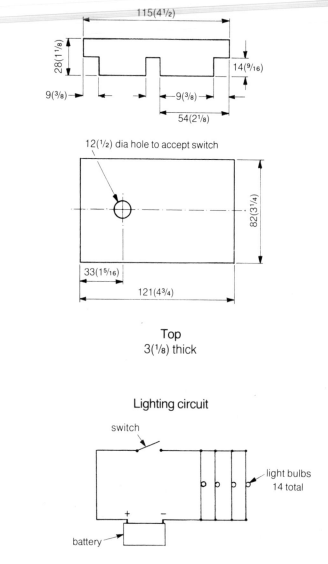

115(4½)

28(1⅛)

14(⁹/₁₆)

9(³/₈)

9(³/₈)

54(2⅛)

12(½) dia hole to accept switch

82(3¼)

33(1⁵/₁₆)

121(4¾)

### Top
3(⅛) thick

### End walls
make two, 9(³/₈) thick

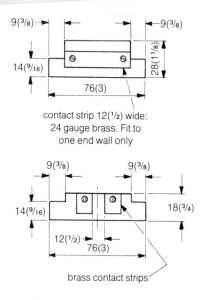

9(³/₈)

9(³/₈)

14(⁹/₁₆)

28(1⅛)

76(3)

contact strip 12(½) wide:
24 gauge brass. Fit to
one end wall only

9(³/₈)

9(³/₈)

14(⁹/₁₆)

18(¾)

12(½)

76(3)

brass contact strips

### Middle wall
9(³/₈) thick

### Middle wall contact strips
make two, 12(½) wide;
24 gauge brass

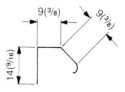

9(³/₈)

9(³/₈)

14(⁹/₁₆)

### Lighting circuit

switch

light bulbs
14 total

+     −

battery

# Fig 10 Positions of airport buildings and grass areas

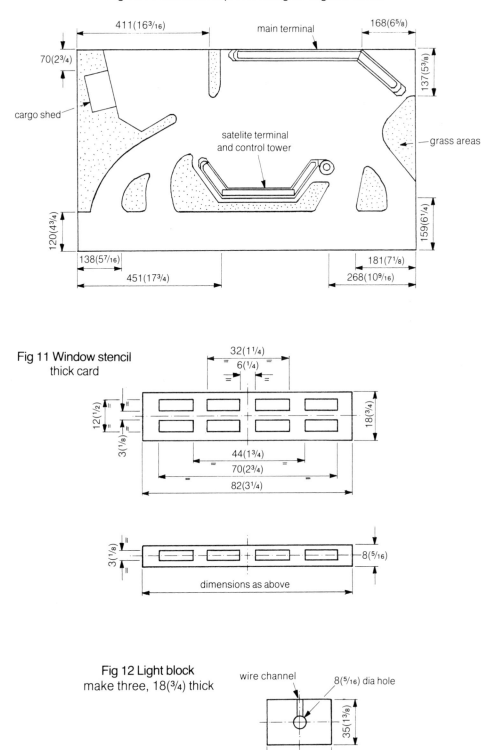

411(16³/₁₆)

main terminal

168(6⁵/₈)

70(2³/₄)

137(5³/₈)

cargo shed

satelite terminal
and control tower

grass areas

120(4³/₄)

159(6¹/₄)

138(5⁷/₁₆)

451(17³/₄)

181(7¹/₈)

268(10⁹/₁₆)

# Fig 11 Window stencil
thick card

32(1¹/₄)

6(¹/₄)

12(¹/₂)

18(³/₄)

3(¹/₈)

44(1³/₄)

70(2³/₄)

82(3¹/₄)

3(¹/₈)

8(⁵/₁₆)

dimensions as above

# Fig 12 Light block
make three, 18(³/₄) thick

wire channel

8(⁵/₁₆) dia hole

35(1³/₈)

50(2)

115

Fig 13 Grass patterns          19(³/₄) squares

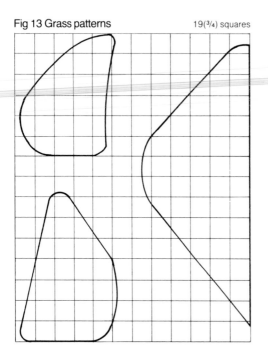

Fig 14 Grass patterns          19(³/₄) squares

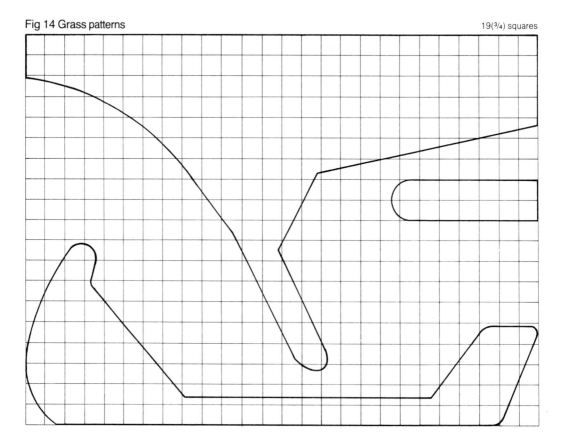

**Cutting list**

| | | | |
|---|---|---|---|
| Base (Fig 1) | 3 off | 1056×35×18mm (41¾×1⅜×¾in) | Wood |
| | 4 off | 610×35×18mm (24×1⅜×¾in) | Wood |
| (Fig 3) | 2 off | 1056×610×3mm (41¾×24×⅛in) | Hardboard |
| Light blocks | 3 off | 50×35×18mm (2×1⅜×¾in) | Wood |
| Main terminal (Fig 4) | 1 off | 412×35×18mm (16¼×1⅜×¾in) | Wood |
| | 1 off | 187×35×18mm (7⅜×1⅜×¾in) | Wood |
| Top battens | 1 off | 388×23×8mm (15⅛×⅞×5/16in) | Wood |
| | 1 off | 162×23×8mm (6⅜×⅞×5/16in) | Wood |
| Satellite terminal (Fig 5) | 2 off | 137×35×18mm (5⅜×1⅜×¾in) | Wood |
| | 1 off | 228×35×18mm (9×1⅜×¾in) | Wood |
| Top battens | 2 off | 110×23×8mm (45/16×⅞×5/16in) | Wood |
| | 1 off | 222×23×8mm (8¾×⅞×5/16in) | Wood |
| Control tower (Fig 7) | make from | 67×45×45mm (2⅜×1¾×1¾in) | Wood |
| | 1 off | 22mm(⅞in)dia×9mm(⅜in)thick | Plywood |
| Battery box (Fig 9) (sides) | 2 off | 115×28×9mm (4½×1⅛×⅜in) | Plywood |
| | 2 off | 76×28×9mm (3×1⅛×⅜in) | Plywood |
| Base | 1 off | 115×76×3mm (4½×3×⅛in) | Plywood |
| Top | 1 off | 121×82×3mm (4¾×3¼×⅛in) | Plywood |
| Top strips | 2 off | 115×9×3mm (4½×⅜×⅛in) | Plywood |
| | 2 off | 82×9×3mm (3¼×⅜×⅛in) | Plywood |
| Middle wall | 1 off | 76×18×9mm (3×¾×⅜in) | Plywood |

*Ancillaries*

| | | |
|---|---|---|
| | 1 off | 58mm(2¼in)long×12mm(½in)wide 24 gauge brass strip |
| | 2 off | 38mm(1in)long×12mm(½in)wide 24 gauge brass strip |
| | 14 off | Runway light lenses 9mm(⅜in)long. These are made from disposable ball-point pens which have transparent stems |
| | | 25×25mm (1×1in) square red acetate sheet |
| | | 95×18mm (3¾×1¼in) clear plastic sheet |
| | | 3000mm (118in) 0.5mm² stranded electrical cable |
| | 1 off | Toggle switch |
| | 14 off | 'Grain of wheat' bulbs |
| | | 1092×646mm (43¼×25½in) black felt |
| | | Model railway scenic 'grass' |
| | 2 off | HP11 batteries |

# RAILWAY

*(shown in colour on page 33)*

This push/pull-along railway has been made so that children can make their own miniature world of trains.

I have included drawings for some of the things that are to be found on a railway, and if more than one of each model is required this can easily be done.

The colours I have chosen are close to the real thing, but don't be afraid to try different colour schemes. If the whole railway or just the engine is required for younger children, then I would suggest a bright colour scheme, as small children like bright shiny colours.

Throughout the method for construc-tion, you will see reference to 1mm($1/32$in) thick plywood; this comes in sheet form and should be available in small quan-tities from model shops as opposed to toy shops.

Plasterboard nails are required for use as buffers in this project to add a touch of realism. These you will find available in most builders' merchants or hardware stores. Because they are galvanised, some of their shafts may be jagged and their heads eccentric. Before fitting them, clean up their shafts with a small file otherwise they will split the wood on entry.

The hooks used to couple the trucks

## Fig 1 Assembled engine

Front view

Side view

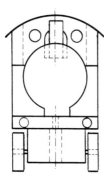
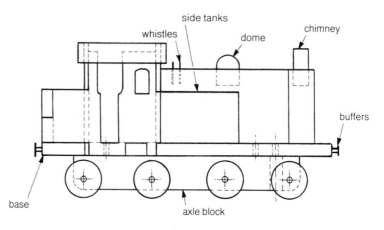

Rear view

Plan view

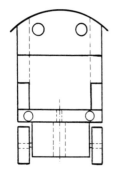
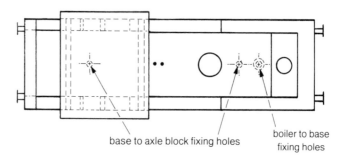

base to axle block fixing holes

boiler to base fixing holes

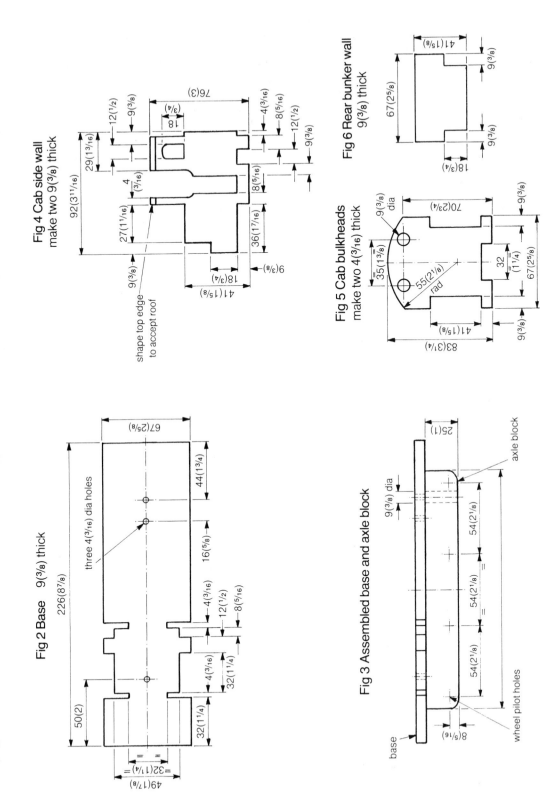

Fig 4 Cab side wall
make two 9($\frac{3}{8}$) thick

76(3)
12($\frac{1}{2}$)
9($\frac{3}{8}$)
18 ($\frac{3}{4}$)
4($\frac{3}{16}$)
8($\frac{5}{16}$)
12($\frac{1}{2}$)
9($\frac{3}{8}$)
29(1$\frac{3}{16}$)
4 ($\frac{3}{16}$)
27(1$\frac{1}{16}$)
8($\frac{5}{16}$)
36(1$\frac{7}{16}$)
92(3$\frac{11}{16}$)
9($\frac{3}{8}$)
18($\frac{3}{4}$)
41(1$\frac{5}{8}$)
9($\frac{3}{8}$)

shape top edge
to accept roof

Fig 6 Rear bunker wall
9($\frac{3}{8}$) thick

41(1$\frac{5}{8}$)
9($\frac{3}{8}$)
67(2$\frac{5}{8}$)
9($\frac{3}{8}$)
18($\frac{3}{4}$)

Fig 5 Cab bulkheads
make two 4($\frac{3}{16}$) thick

9($\frac{3}{8}$) dia
70(2$\frac{3}{4}$)
9($\frac{3}{8}$)
35(1$\frac{3}{8}$)
32 (1$\frac{1}{4}$)
67(2$\frac{5}{8}$)
55(2$\frac{1}{8}$) rad
41(1$\frac{5}{8}$)
9($\frac{3}{8}$)
83(3$\frac{1}{4}$)

Fig 2 Base   9($\frac{3}{8}$) thick

67(2$\frac{5}{8}$)
44(1$\frac{3}{4}$)
three 4($\frac{3}{16}$) dia holes
16($\frac{5}{8}$)
226(8$\frac{7}{8}$)
4($\frac{3}{16}$)
12($\frac{1}{2}$)
8($\frac{5}{16}$)
50(2)
4($\frac{3}{16}$)
32(1$\frac{1}{4}$)
32(1$\frac{1}{4}$)
32(1$\frac{1}{4}$)
49(1$\frac{7}{8}$)

Fig 3 Assembled base and axle block

25(1)
axle block
9($\frac{3}{8}$) dia
54(2$\frac{1}{8}$)
54(2$\frac{1}{8}$)
54(2$\frac{1}{8}$)
base
18($\frac{5}{16}$)
wheel pilot holes

together are of the same type that are used to hang net curtains, and should be available from hardware stores or the fabric departments of other stores.

For simplification of the drawings, the wheels are only shown on the engine plans and the buffer and hook positions are only shown on the goods truck drawings, but they are the same throughout the project.

*Engine*

1 Mark and cut out the base (Fig 2). Mark out the 4mm($^3$/16in) dia holes, drill and countersink. The countersink side is now the upper face.

2 Mark and cut out the axle block (Fig 3),

making sure to mark out and drill the pilot holes for the wheels before rounding off the lower edges. Drill a 9mm ($^3$/8in) hole as shown. This will be used to secure the boiler to the base at a later stage.

3 Do not be tempted to join the base and axle block together at this stage, but wait until all cab walls have been test assembled on base and fit correctly.

4 Mark and cut out all cab walls, bulkheads and rear bunker wall (Figs 4, 5 and 6).

5 Place the two cab bulkhead walls back to back, to make sure that the roof curve is the same. If they differ in shape, secure them firmly together in a vice or to the

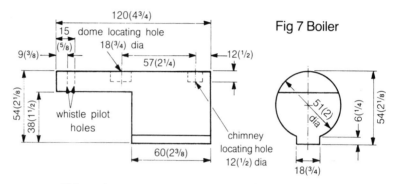

Fig 7 Boiler

Side tanks   make two 60 × 38 × 25(2⅜ × 1½ × 1)

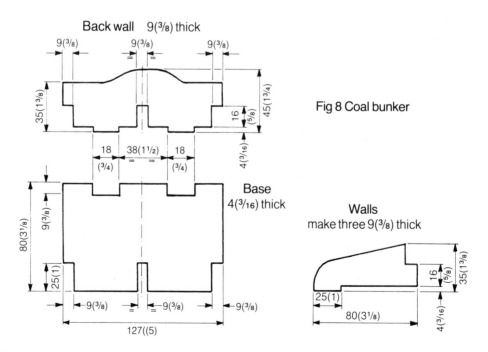

Fig 8 Coal bunker

Back wall   9(³/8) thick

Base
4(³/16) thick

Walls
make three 9(³/8) thick

bench with cramps, and using a small file or glass paper wrapped around a sanding block, shape them so that they are both the same.

6 Test assemble all the parts you now have and clean out joints where needed. Joints have to be a tight fit for strength, so do not remove too much with the file before checking the fit again.

7 When satisfied that the walls are a nice tight fit in the base, place the base in position on the axle block, and mark through the base fitting holes. Drill pilot holes in the axle block where the marks are.

8 Now the axle block and base can be screwed and glued together.

9 For final assembly of the cab, it is important that the front and rear bulkheads are glued into place first, followed by the side walls and rear bunker wall. Wipe off any excess glue with a damp cloth.

10 Mark and cut out the boiler and boiler side tanks (Figs 7 and 8).

11 If you don't have any wood the exact size of the boiler, don't worry because two pieces can be glued together to give an approximate size and reduced when shaping. Always cramp pieces of wood to be joined until the glue has dried.

12 Before any shaping of the boiler can begin, it is important to mark out and drill holes for the chimney and dome (Fig 9); and pilot holes for the whistle and safety valve. If an electrical drilling machine is used for this purpose a flat or zip bit (*see* page 13) will be needed. A drill stand will be a great help here to gauge the exact depth. If you do not have one there is another way. Measure the depth required against the drill bit to be used and wrap a small piece of PVC insulating tape around the drill bit at this point. This is now your depth gauge.

13 Mark out the boiler shape using a compass and pencil on both ends of the boiler. Mark out the square portion to be removed on the rear of the boiler. Mark all waste areas of the wood with a pencil.

14 Secure the boiler and remove the waste wood at the rear using a tenon saw. Clean out the cut with a sharp chisel so that the boiler side tanks fit snugly underneath when placed on a flat surface.

15 Using a sharp hand plane we can now shape the boiler. If a vice is not available to secure the boiler while shaping is in progress, screw a piece of waste plywood to the bottom of the boiler and cramp this to the bench.

16 It will be found that not all of the shaping can be done with a plane. The remainder will have to be done using a large, sharp, flat chisel with the boiler upside down. To secure the boiler in this position without a vice, screw your piece of spare plywood through the holes you have made for the chimney and dome.

17 When you have finished shaping with hand plane and chisel, use sandpaper to smooth off.

18 Glue the boiler side tanks in position and when dried, glue and screw the boiler in position, adding the dome and chimney. Shape the dome before separating it from its original length of dowel (ie before cutting it to length).

19 Using a sharp craft knife and steel rule (not a tape measure) mark and cut out the two pieces of 1mm ($^1/_{32}$in) thick plywood that will be used for the cab roof. Mark a border of 4mm ($^3/_{16}$in) all around the edges of one piece; this is the overlap.

20 The fixing of the roof to the cab requires two pieces of waste wood slightly longer than the cab, and at least two lengths of PVC tape long enough to go all around the engine. Prepare these items before attempting to glue the first roof section in position. Spread glue all around the top of the cab walls, place the first roof section in place and position the two pieces of spare wood over the outside walls of the cab pressing down on the roof section. Next, wrap the PVC tape around the engine making sure that the spare wood stays in place. When this has been done glue the second roof on top of the first. This can be secured to the first roof by large bulldog paper clips around the side edges. Leave until dry, then tidy up edges.

21 Screw two $^1/_2$in No4 brass wood screws into the pilot holes, already drilled, for the safety valve and whistle until the shank of the screw just starts to disappear. Carefully cut the heads off the screws with a junior hacksaw, and gently round off the screw shank with a small file. Any sharp edge, no matter how small, will catch a

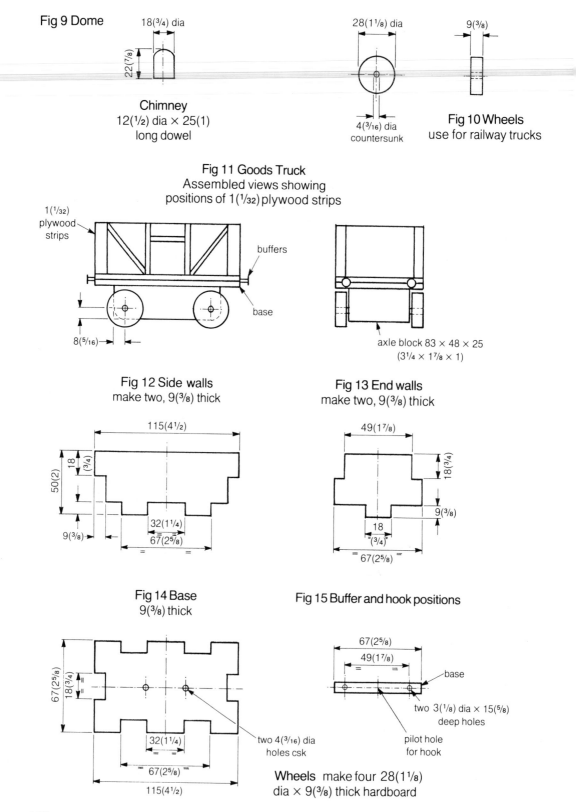

Fig 9 Dome

18(¾) dia

22(⅞)

28(1⅛) dia

9(⅜)

Chimney
12(½) dia × 25(1)
long dowel

4(³⁄₁₆) dia
countersunk

Fig 10 Wheels
use for railway trucks

Fig 11 Goods Truck
Assembled views showing
positions of 1(¹⁄₃₂) plywood strips

1(¹⁄₃₂)
plywood
strips

buffers

base

8(⁵⁄₁₆)

axle block 83 × 48 × 25
(3¼ × 1⅞ × 1)

Fig 12 Side walls
make two, 9(⅜) thick

115(4½)

50(2)

18
(¾)

9(⅜)

32(1¼)

67(2⅝)

Fig 13 End walls
make two, 9(⅜) thick

49(1⅞)

18(¾)

9(⅜)

18
(¾)

67(2⅝)

Fig 14 Base
9(⅜) thick

67(2⅝)

18(¾)

32(1¼)

67(2⅝)

115(4½)

two 4(³⁄₁₆) dia
holes csk

Fig 15 Buffer and hook positions

67(2⅝)

49(1⅞)

base

two 3(⅛) dia × 15(⅝)
deep holes

pilot hole
for hook

Wheels make four 28(1⅛)
dia × 9(⅜) thick hardboard

child's small fingers.

22 Mark and drill pilot holes for buffers and hooks.

23 Using a hole saw that will give an inside dia of 28mm (1⅛in), cut out eight wheels (Fig 10) for the engine and any others that you need for trucks, from 9mm (⅜in) thick hardwood.

24 If the drill bit with the hole saw is in excess of 4mm (³/₁₆in) dia, drill out the wheel centre to 9mm (⅜in) dia and insert a 9mm (⅜in) length of 9mm (⅜in) dia dowel rod. Redrill the dowel in the centre with a 4mm (³/₁₆in) dia hole, to accept the wheel fixing screw. This is not an exact science so a little care has to be taken.

25 When fitting the wheels, place a washer, which has an inside dia of 4mm (³/₁₆in), on the inside face. Do not over tighten the wheel screws, slacken them until the wheels run freely.

26 Gently, using a small hammer, tap the buffers into position and screw the hooks into their previously drilled pilot holes.

27 When painting, always use paints that are safe for children.

28 Now you are ready to start your next project.

*Coal bunker*

1 To make the coal bunker cut out and assemble as shown in Fig 8.

*Goods truck*

1 Mark and cut out all parts (Figs 11–15).
2 When marking out joints use a pencil to shade areas to be removed. It is so easy to remove the wrong pieces.

3 Mark wheel positions on axle block and drill pilot holes.

4 Mark and drill two 4mm (³/₁₆in) holes in base and countersink them.

5 Test assemble all walls on to base and clean out joints with a file where needed.

6 Glue walls to the base, use cramps until dry.

7 Screw and glue axle block to base.

8 Mark, cut out and glue into position 1mm (¹/₃₂in) thick plywood strips on to the wall sides.

9 Drill pilot holes for buffers and hooks and fit them in position.

10 Cut out and fit wheels as described in engine construction (sections 23–25, see above).

*Goods van*

1 Mark and cut out all parts (Figs 17–19).
2 Mark wheel positions on axle block and drill pilot holes.

3 Mark and drill two 4mm (³/₁₆in) holes in base.

4 Place the two end walls back to back and check that the curves are both the same. Reshape if required.

5 Dry assemble walls to base, cleaning joints where needed. Tight joints are always better than sloppy ones, so take care.

6 Glue and screw axle block to base.

7 Using a steel rule, or other form of straight edge, check how much of the side wall's top edge has to be removed so that

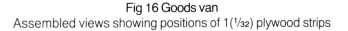

Fig 16 Goods van
Assembled views showing positions of 1(¹/₃₂) plywood strips

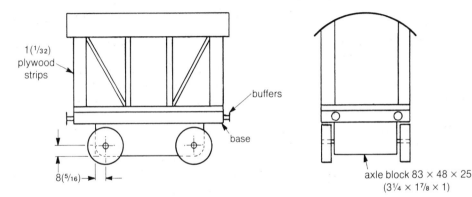

1(¹/₃₂) plywood strips

buffers

base

8(⁵/₁₆)

axle block 83 × 48 × 25
(3¼ × 1⅞ × 1)

123

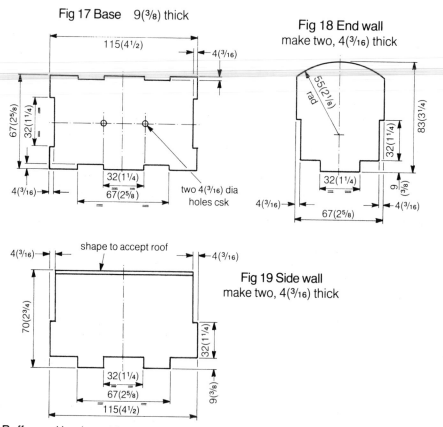

Fig 17 Base   9(³/8) thick

115(4½)

4(³/16)

67(2⁵/8)

32(1¼)

4(³/16)

32(1¼)

67(2⁵/8)

two 4(³/16) dia
holes csk

Fig 18 End wall
make two, 4(³/16) thick

55(2⅛) rad

32(1¼)

83(3¼)

32(1¼)

9
(³/8)

4(³/16)

67(2⁵/8)

4(³/16)

shape to accept roof

4(³/16)

4(³/16)

Fig 19 Side wall
make two, 4(³/16) thick

70(2³/4)

32(1¼)

32(1¼)

67(2⁵/8)

115(4½)

9(³/8)

Buffer and hook positions as goods truck
Wheels   make four 28(1⅛) dia × 9(³/8) thick hardwood

the roof will fit correctly. Using sandpaper or a small file, shape this edge, checking as it is done.

8 Mark and cut out the two roof panels and assemble roof as described in engine construction, sections 19–20, page 121.

9 Mark and drill pilot holes for buffers and hooks, and fit same.

10 Using the drawing as a guide, mark and cut out the 1mm (¹/32in) thick plywood strips and glue in position.

11 Cut out and fit wheels as described in engine construction, sections 23–25 (*see* page 123).

*Guard's van*

1 Mark and cut out all walls (Figs 21–23).

2 Mark window positions on all end walls and remove waste plywood as described in methods (page 9).

3 Mark and cut out base (Fig 24). Cut slots for walls. Drill and countersink two 4mm

(³/16in) dia holes.

4 Test assemble all walls on to base.

5 Place all end walls back to back and check that the roof curves are the same. Smooth off if needed.

6 Mark and drill pilot holes for wheels in axle block, and pilot holes for buffers and hooks in base.

7 Screw and glue axle block to base.

8 Glue all walls to base and cramp until dried.

9 Using a steel rule or other form of straight edge, check that there are no high spots on the roof curve now that the end walls are in position. If there are, take them out until all walls have the same curve.

10 Assemble roof as described in engine construction, sections 19–20, page 121.

11 Fit buffers, hooks and wheels in position. To make wheels refer to engine construction, sections 23–25, page 123.

## Fig 20 Guard's van
Assembled views

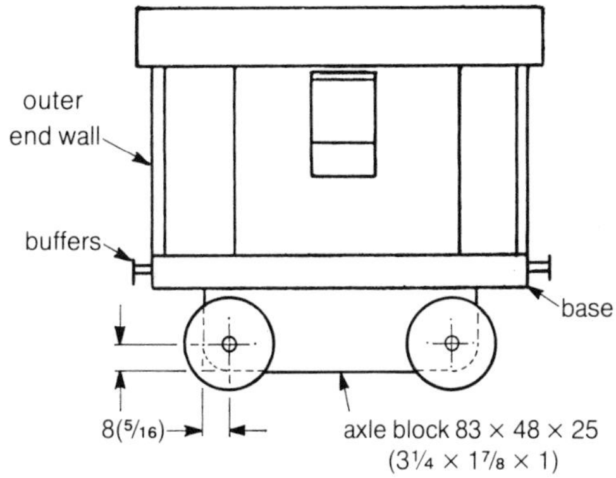
outer
end wall
buffers
base
8(5/16)
axle block 83 × 48 × 25
(3 1/4 × 1 7/8 × 1)

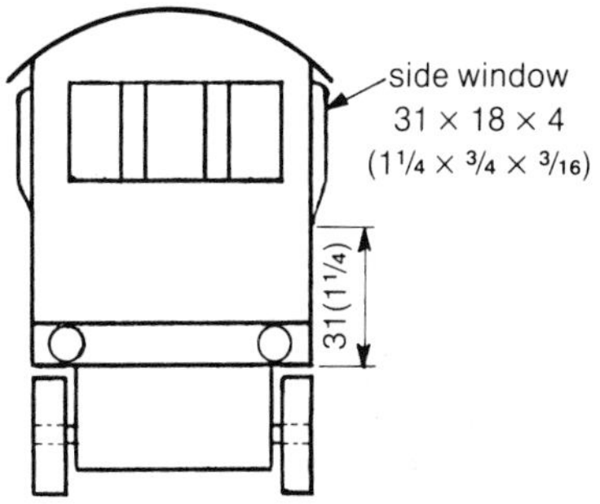
side window
31 × 18 × 4
(1 1/4 × 3/4 × 3/16)
31(1 1/4)

## Fig 21 Side wall
make two, 4(3/16) thick

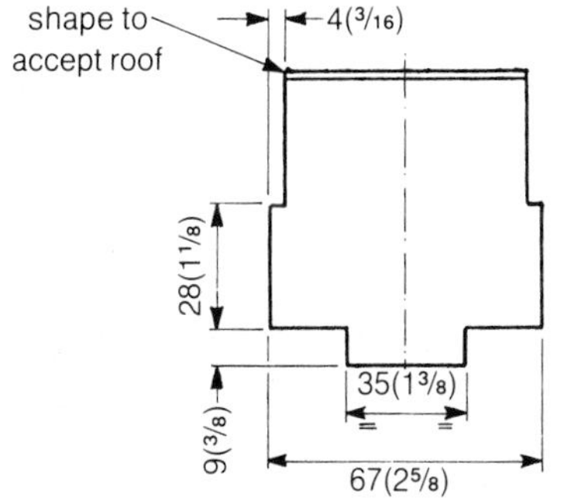
shape to
accept roof
4(3/16)
28(1 1/8)
9(3/8)
35(1 3/8)
67(2 5/8)

## Fig 22 Cabin end wall
make two,
4(3/16) thick

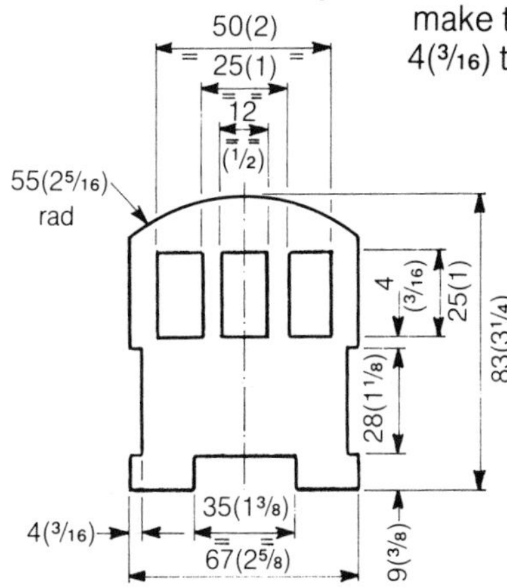
50(2)
25(1)
12
(1/2)
55(2 5/16)
rad
4
(3/16)
25(1)
83(3 1/4)
28(1 1/8)
35(1 3/8)
4(3/16)
67(2 5/8)
9(3/8)

## Fig 23 Outer end wall
make two, 4(3/16) thick

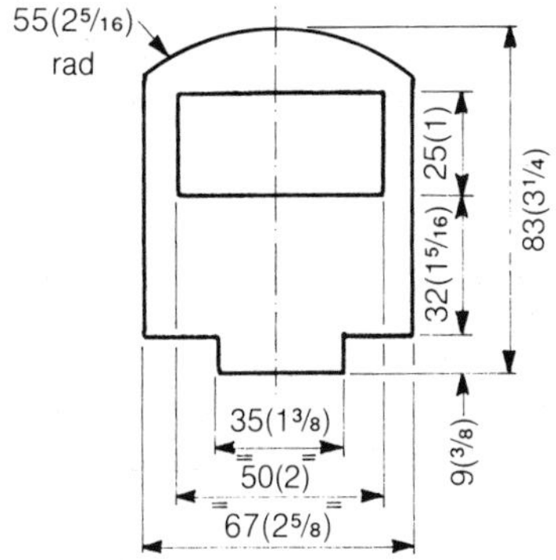
55(2 5/16)
rad
25(1)
32(1 5/16)
83(3 1/4)
35(1 3/8)
50(2)
67(2 5/8)
9(3/8)

## Fig 24 Base
9(3/8) thick

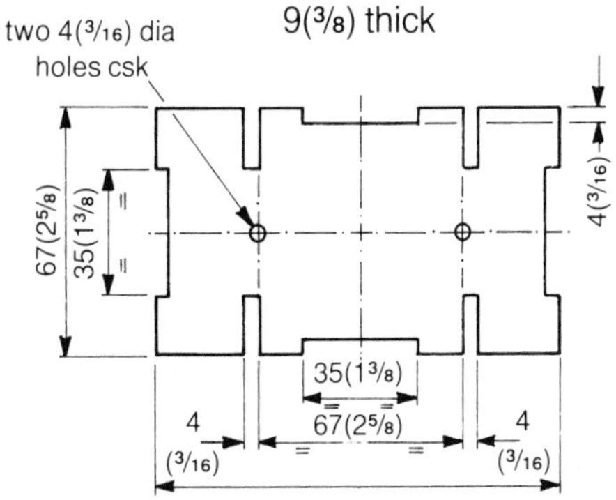
two 4(3/16) dia
holes csk
67(2 5/8)
35(1 3/8)
4(3/16)
35(1 3/8)
67(2 5/8)
4
(3/16)
4
(3/16)

**Buffer and hook positions as goods truck**

**Wheels** make four 28(1 1/8) dia × 9(3/8) thick hardwood

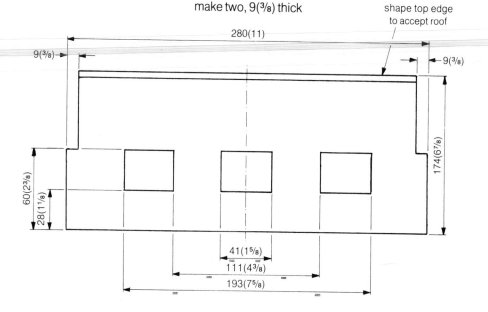

**Fig 25 Engine shed side wall**
make two, 9(³/₈) thick

shape top edge
to accept roof

280(11)

9(³/₈)

9(³/₈)

60(2³/₈)

28(1¹/₈)

174(6⁷/₈)

41(1⁵/₈)

111(4³/₈)

193(7⁵/₈)

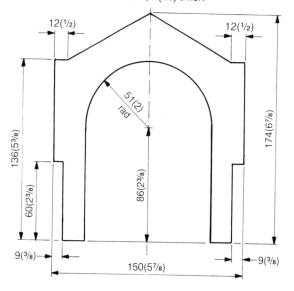

**Fig 26 End wall**
make two, 9(³/₈) thick

12(¹/₂)

12(¹/₂)

51(2) rad

136(5³/₈)

60(2³/₈)

86(2³/₈)

174(6⁷/₈)

9(³/₈)

9(³/₈)

150(5⁷/₈)

*Engine shed*
1 Mark and cut out the two side walls (Fig 25), and test assemble the whole thing.
2 Mark out the two end walls (Fig 26), but cut out the arch before cutting the outside shape.
3 Cut window openings.
4 Glue walls together, checking that they are 90° to each other with a try-square and secure with cramps until dry.
5 Cut to length 9mm (³/₈in)² wood for roof supports and fix to end walls as shown in drawing (Fig 28). Use the top edge of the side walls as a guide. The roof pitch (angle) is 30°.
6 Cut to length and glue 9mm (³/₈in)² wood to the inside corners.
7 Using the roof support wood as a guide, file off the top inside edges of the side walls. Test fit the roof frequently.
8 When you have shaped the top inside edges of both side walls, glue the roof in position.
9 Sand or file the outside edges of the roof until they are vertical.
10 Mark and cut out capping stones from 3mm (¹/₈in) thick plywood, and glue into position. Shape the edges so that they fit well.

## Fig 27 Engine shed
### Assembled views

Side view

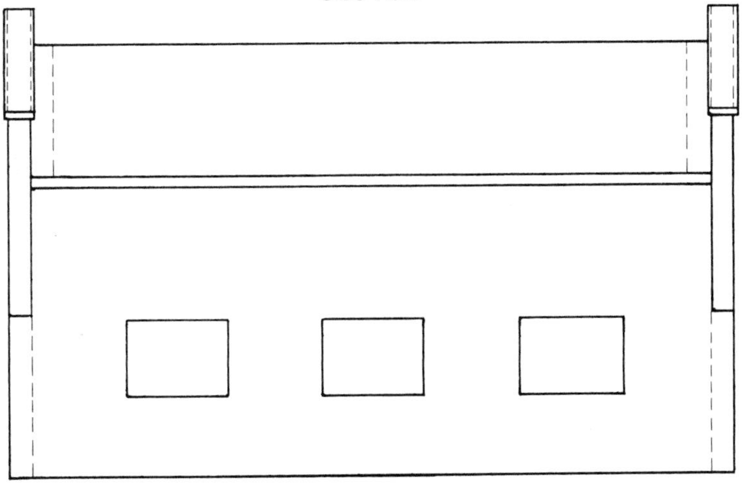

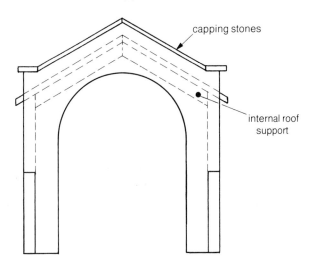

## Fig 28 Front view
### Internal roof supports shown

capping stones

internal roof
support

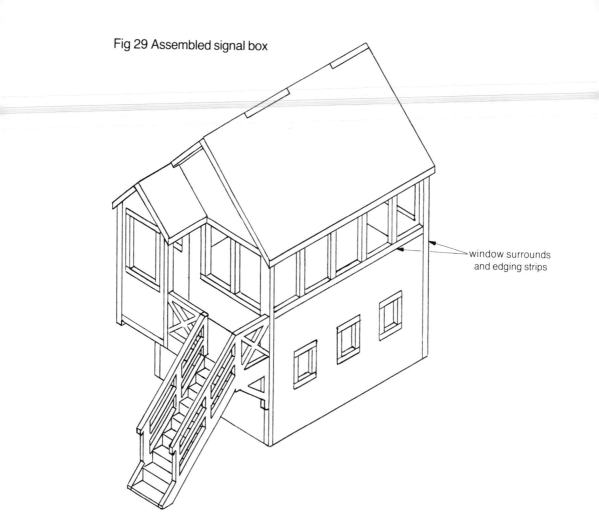

Fig 29 Assembled signal box

window surrounds
and edging strips

*Signal box*
1 Mark and cut out the front wall (Fig 30).
Carefully cut out the window and hand
rail openings. Use a very small file to clean
up the hand rail openings.
2 Mark and cut out the remaining three
walls (Figs 31 and 32) and test assemble.
3 Place the end walls back to back and
check that the roof edges are the same.
4 Cut 9mm (³⁄₈in)² wood to length and glue
one to each wall for the floor supports.
5 Now glue the four main walls and floor
together.
6 Mark and cut out the porch wall (Fig 33),
porch roof (Fig 34), balcony (Fig 35) and
middle balcony support bracket (Fig 36).

Test assemble and glue in position.
7 After making the hand rail on the front
wall, making the second hand rail (Fig 37)
will be straightforward. Use the first as a
stencil. When finished smooth off the
edges and glue in position.
8 Cut out and glue to the underneath of the
hand rails a piece of 85×33×1mm
(3³⁄₈×1⁵⁄₁₆×¹⁄₃₂in) thick plywood. This
will be used to glue the steps (Fig 38).
9 Cut seven 25mm (1in) lengths of 9mm
(³⁄₈in)² wood for the steps. Mark a diagonal
pencil line on each end face and using a
small plane remove one half to leave a
triangle shape. Test assemble and glue
steps in position.

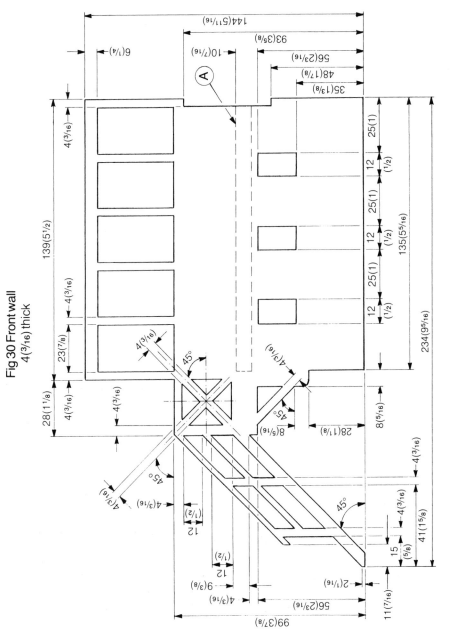

Fig 30 Front wall
4($^3/_{16}$) thick

A = Floor fixing batten 131 × 9 × 9(5$^1/_8$ × $^3/_8$ × $^3/_8$)

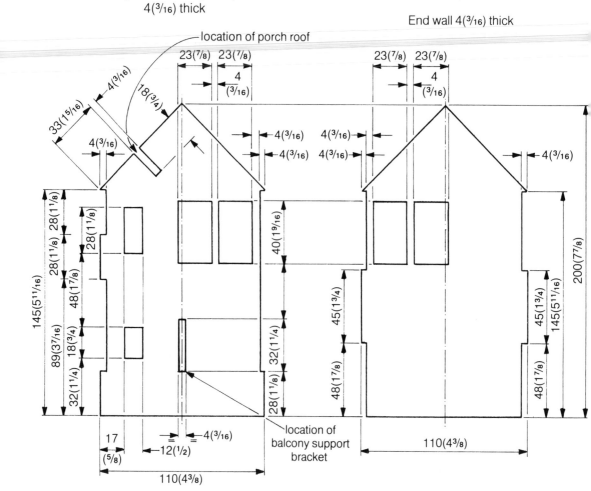

Fig 31 End wall (porch)
4(³/₁₆) thick

End wall 4(³/₁₆) thick

10 It is best to glue the roof sections (Fig 39) together, separate from the rest of the building. This is because a 9mm (³/₈in)² piece of wood is glued across the join for strength. It is also advisable at this point to paint the inside before the roof is glued into position. I painted all of the walls with a cream emulsion.

11 Before glueing the assembled roof in position, mark a border along the outside edge of the front roof 6mm (¹/₄in) wide. This will allow for the overlap.

12 Using the drawing (Fig 29) as a guide, cut out 4mm (³/₁₆in) wide strips of 1mm (¹/₃₂in) thick plywood and glue them in position around the windows and vertical corners of the signal box. These strips will aid painting quite considerably.

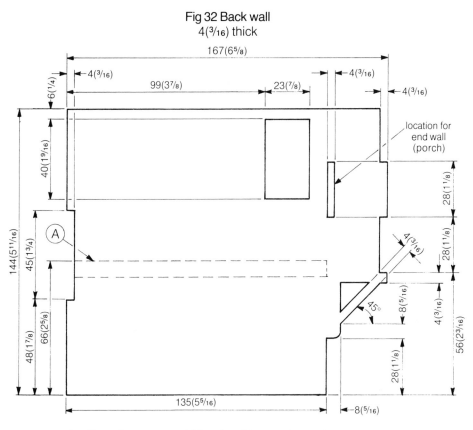

Fig 32 Back wall
4($^3/_{16}$) thick

167(6$^5/_8$)

4($^3/_{16}$)
99(3$^7/_8$)
23($^7/_8$)
4($^3/_{16}$)
4($^3/_{16}$)
6($^1/_4$)

location for
end wall
(porch)

40(1$^9/_{16}$)

28(1$^1/_8$)

144(5$^{11}/_{16}$)
45(1$^3/_4$)

A

28(1$^1/_8$)

4($^3/_{16}$)

4($^3/_{16}$)

45°

8($^5/_{16}$)

56(2$^3/_{16}$)

48(1$^7/_8$)
66(2$^5/_8$)

28(1$^1/_8$)

135(5$^5/_{16}$)

8($^5/_{16}$)

A = Floor fixing batten 131 × 9 × 9(5$^1/_8$ × $^3/_8$ × $^3/_8$)

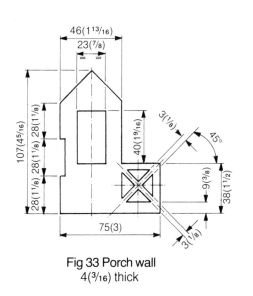

46(1$^{13}/_{16}$)
23($^7/_8$)

107(4$^5/_{16}$)
28(1$^1/_8$) 28(1$^1/_8$) 28(1$^1/_8$)

40(1$^9/_{16}$)

3($^1/_8$)
45°

9($^3/_8$)
38(1$^1/_2$)

75(3)
3($^1/_8$)

Fig 33 Porch wall
4($^3/_{16}$) thick

Fig 34 Porch roof
4($^3/_{16}$) thick

38(1$^9/_{16}$)

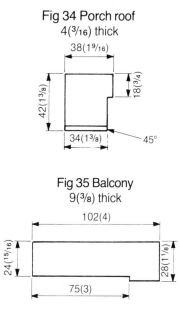

42(1$^3/_8$)

18($^3/_4$)

34(1$^3/_8$)

45°

Fig 35 Balcony
9($^3/_8$) thick

102(4)

24($^{15}/_{16}$)

28(1$^1/_8$)

75(3)

131

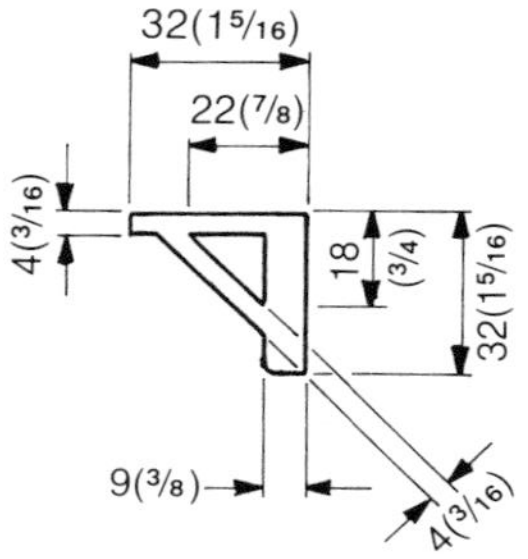

32(1⁵/₁₆)
22(⁷/₈)
4(³/₁₆)
18
(³/₄)
32(1⁵/₁₆)
9(³/₈)
4(³/₁₆)


Fig 36 Balcony support bracket
4(³/₁₆) thick

Fig 37 Stair hand rail
4(³/₁₆) thick

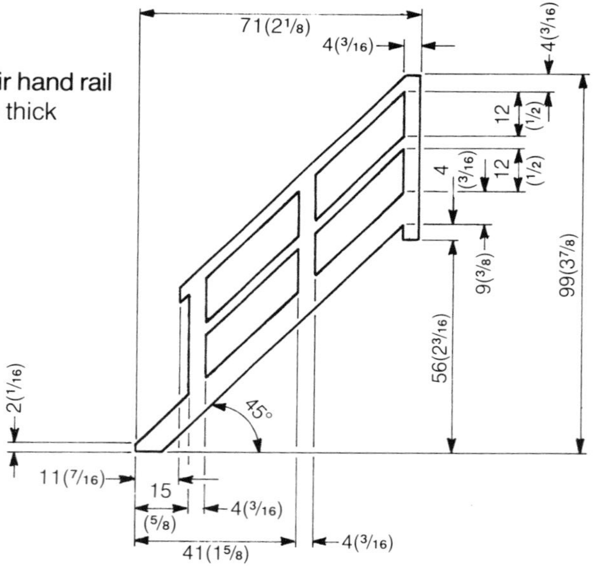

71(2¹/₈)
4(³/₁₆)
4(³/₁₆)
12
(¹/₂)
4
(³/₁₆)
12
(¹/₂)
9(³/₈)
99(3⁷/₈)
56(2³/₁₆)
45°
2(¹/₁₆)
11(⁷/₁₆)
15
(⁵/₈)
4(³/₁₆)
41(1⁵/₈)
4(³/₁₆)


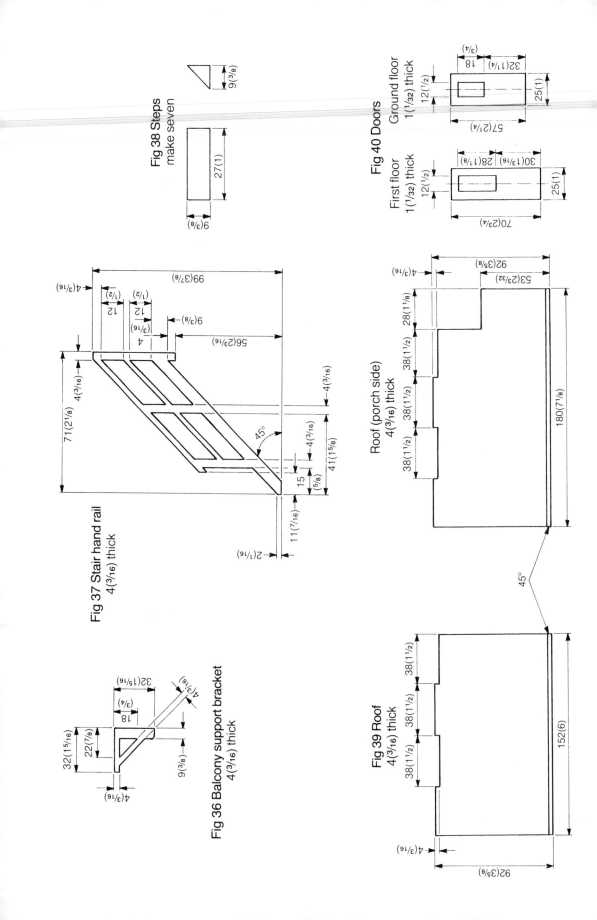

Fig 38 Steps
make seven

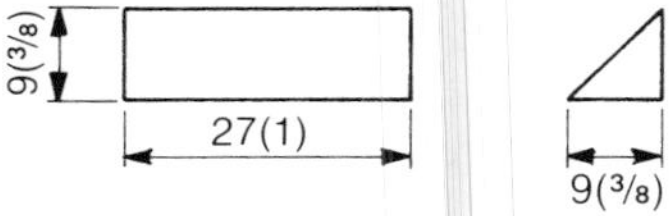

9(³/₈)
27(1)
9(³/₈)


Fig 39 Roof
4(³/₁₆) thick

Roof (porch side)
4(³/₁₆) thick

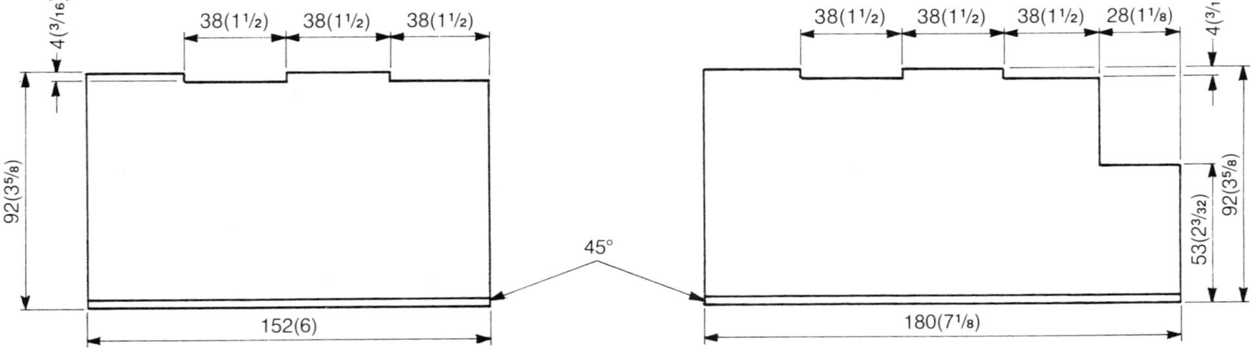

38(1¹/₂)
38(1¹/₂)
38(1¹/₂)
4(³/₁₆)
92(3⁵/₈)
152(6)
45°
38(1¹/₂)
38(1¹/₂)
38(1¹/₂)
28(1¹/₈)
4(³/₁₆)
53(2³/₃₂)
92(3⁵/₈)
180(7¹/₈)


Fig 40 Doors

First floor
1(¹/₃₂) thick

Ground floor
1(¹/₃₂) thick

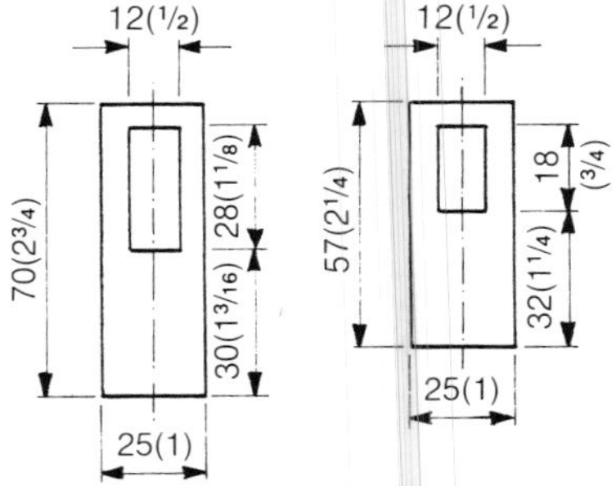

12(¹/₂)
70(2³/₄)
28(1¹/₈)
30(1³/₁₆)
25(1)
12(¹/₂)
57(2¹/₄)
18
(³/₄)
32(1¹/₄)
25(1)

**Cutting list**

*Engine*

| | | | |
|---|---|---|---|
| Axle block (Fig 3) | 1 off | 178×48×25mm (7×1⅞×1in) | Wood |
| Base (Fig 2) | 1 off | 226×67×9mm (8⅞×2⅝×⅜in) | Plywood |
| Cab side walls (Fig 4) | 2 off | 92×76×9mm (3¹¹/₁₆×3×⅜in) | Plywood |
| Rear bunker wall (Fig 6) | 1 off | 67×41×9mm (2⅝×1⅝×⅜in) | Plywood |
| Cab bulkheads (Fig 5) | 2 off | 67×83×4mm (2⅝×3¼×³/₁₆in) | Plywood |
| Side tanks (Fig 8) | 2 off | 60×38×25mm (2⅜×1½×1in) | Wood |
| Boiler (Fig 7) | 1 off | 120×54×51mm (4¾×2⅛×2in) | Wood |
| Dome (Fig 9) | 1 off | 18mm(¾in)dia×22mm(⅞in)long dowel | |
| Chimney | 1 off | 12mm(½in)dia×25mm(1in)long dowel | |
| Cab roof | 2 off | 67×88×1mm (2⅝×3½×¹/₃₂in) | Plywood |
| Wheels (Fig 10) | 8 off | 28mm(1⅛in)dia×9mm(⅜in)thick | Wood |
| Safety valves | 2 off | ½in×No4 brass wood screws | |
| Coupling hooks | 2 off | Net curtain hooks | |
| Buffers | 4 off | Plasterboard nails cut to 18mm(¾in) long with a head of approx 9mm(⅜in) | |

*Goods truck*

| | | | |
|---|---|---|---|
| Axle block (Fig 3) | 1 off | 83×48×25mm (3¼×1⅞×1in) | Wood |
| Base (Fig 14) | 1 off | 115×67×9mm (4½×2⅝×⅜in) | Plywood |
| Side walls (Fig 12) | 2 off | 115×50×9mm (4½×2×⅜in) | Plywood |
| End walls (Fig 13) | 2 off | 67×50×9mm (2⅝×2×⅜in) | Plywood |
| Wheels (Fig 10) | 4 off | As engine | |
| Coupling hooks (Fig 15) | 2 off | As engine | |
| Buffers (Fig 15) | 4 off | As engine | |

Various lengths 1mm(¹/₃₂in) thick plywood strips, *see* Fig 11.

*Goods van*

| | | | |
|---|---|---|---|
| Axle block (Fig 3) | 1 off | 83×48×25mm (3¼×1⅞×1in) | Wood |
| Base (Fig 17) | 1 off | 115×67×9mm (4½×2⅝×⅜in) | Plywood |
| Side walls (Fig 19) | 2 off | 115×70×4mm (4½×2¾×³/₁₆in) | Plywood |
| End walls (Fig 18) | 2 off | 83×67×4mm (3¼×2⅝×³/₁₆in) | Plywood |
| Roof | 2 off | 124×88×1mm (4⅞×3½×¹/₃₂in) | Plywood |
| Wheels (Fig 10) | 4 off | As engine | |
| Coupling hooks | 2 off | As engine | |
| Buffers (Fig 15) | 4 off | As engine | |

Various lengths 1mm(¹/₃₂in) thick plywood strips, *see* Fig 16.

*Guard's van*

| | | | |
|---|---|---|---|
| Axle block (Fig 3) | 1 off | 83×48×25mm (3¼×1⅞×1in) | Wood |
| Base (Fig 24) | 1 off | 115×67×9mm (4½×2⅝×⅜in) | Plywood |
| End walls (Figs 22 and 23) | 4 off | 83×67×4mm (3¼×2⅝×³/₁₆in) | Plywood |
| Side walls (Fig 21) | 2 off | 70×67×4mm (2¾×2⅝×³/₁₆in) | Plywood |
| Roof | 2 off | 124×88×1mm (4⅞×3½×¹/₃₂in) | Plywood |
| Wheels (Fig 10) | 4 off | As engine | |
| Coupling hooks | 2 off | As engine | |
| Buffers (Fig 15) | 4 off | As engine | |
| Side windows | 2 off | 32×18×4mm (1¼×¾×³/₁₆in) | Plywood |

## Coal bunker

| | | | |
|---|---|---|---|
| Base (Fig 8) | 1 off | 127×80×4mm (5×3⅛×³⁄₁₆in) | Plywood |
| Back wall (Fig 8) | 1 off | 127×45×9mm (5×1¾×⅜in) | Plywood |
| Dividing walls (Fig 8) | 3 off | 80×35×9mm (3⅛×1⅜×⅜in) | Plywood |

## Engine shed

| | | | |
|---|---|---|---|
| End walls (Fig 26) | 2 off | 174×150×9mm (6⅞×5⅞×⅜in) | Plywood |
| Side walls (Fig 27) | 2 off | 280×120×9mm (11×4¾×⅜in) | Plywood |
| Roof | 2 off | 98×262×4mm (3⅞×10¼×³⁄₁₆in) | Plywood |
| Capping stones | | Make from 3mm (⅛in) thick ×12mm (½in) wide plywood | |
| Corner blocks | 4 off | 57×9×9mm (2¼×⅜×⅜in) | Wood |

## Signal box

| | | | |
|---|---|---|---|
| Front wall (Fig 30) | 1 off | 234×144×4mm (9⁵⁄₁₆×5¹¹⁄₁₆×³⁄₁₆in) | Plywood |
| Back wall (Fig 32) | 1 off | 167×144×4mm (6⅝×5¹¹⁄₁₆×³⁄₁₆in) | Plywood |
| End walls (Fig 31 | 2 off | 110×200×4mm (4⅜×7⅞×³⁄₁₆in) | Plywood |
| Porch wall (Fig 33) | 1 off | 107×75×4mm (4⁵⁄₁₆×3×³⁄₁₆in) | Plywood |
| Balcony (Fig 35) | 1 off | 102×28×9mm (4×1⅛×⅜in) | Wood |
| Balcony support bracket (Fig 36) | 1 off | 32×32×4mm (1⁵⁄₁₆×1⁵⁄₁₆×³⁄₁₆in) | Plywood |
| Hand rail (Fig 37) | make from | 98×71×4mm (3⅞×2⅞×³⁄₁₆in) | Plywood |
| Steps (Fig 38) | 7 off | 27×9×9mm (1×⅜×⅜in) | Wood |
| | 1 off | 27×9×3mm (1×⅜×⅛in) | Plywood |
| | 1 off | 85×35×1mm (3⁵⁄₁₆×1⅜×¹⁄₁₆in) | Plywood |
| Floor | 1 off | 131×102×3mm (5⅛×3¹⁵⁄₁₆×⅛in) | Plywood |
| Roofs; No 1 (Fig 39) | 1 off | 152×92×4mm (6×3⅝×³⁄₁₆in) | Plywood |
| No 2 (Fig 39) | 1 off | 180×92×4mm (7⅛×3⅝×³⁄₁₆in) | Plywood |
| Porch roof (Fig 34) | 1 off | 42×38×4mm (1¾×1⁹⁄₁₆×³⁄₁₆in) | Plywood |
| Door, first floor (Fig 40) | 1 off | 70×25×1mm (2¾×1×¹⁄₁₆in) | Plywood |
| Door, ground floor (Fig 40) | 1 off | 57×25×1mm (2¼×1×¹⁄₁₆in) | Plywood |
| Floor fixing battens | 2 off | 131×9×9mm (5⅛×⅜×⅜in) | Wood |
| Window and door surrounds and edging strips | | Make from 1mm(¹⁄₃₂in) thick plywood | |